TECHNICAL WRITING

DANTES/DSST* Study Guide

© 2016 Breely Crush Publishing, LLC

DSST is a registered trademark of The Thomson Corporation and its affiliated companies, and does not endorse this book.

971121715143

Published by Breely Crush Publishing, LLC
10808 River Front Parkway
South Jordan, UT 84095
www.breelycrushpublishing.com

ISBN-10: 1-61433-176-6
ISBN-13: 978-1-61433-176-6

Printed and bound in the United States of America.

*DSST is a registered trademark of The Thomson Corporation and its affiliated companies, and does not endorse this book.

Table of Contents

Theory and Practice of Technical Writing

The term "technical writing" refers to documents prepared to help a relatively large but specific group of readers make a decision, perform a task, or learn about a topic. Examples of technical writing include:

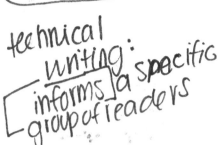

technical writing: informs a specific group of readers

- Software documentation
- Laboratory reports
- Project specifications
- Training modules
- Assembly instructions
- Operations manuals
- Help files
- Journal articles

Technical writing skills are important in many professions. For example, managers need to be able to communicate project objectives and inform subordinates about policy and procedure changes. Engineers must prepare project specifications. Computer programmers may need to document the applications they create.

ESTABLISHING GOALS

GOAL: define objectives

When writing technical material, the first goal is to define objectives for the finished document. These goals will guide the format and language of the document, and serve as benchmarks to gauge the document's completeness and quality.

When determining the goals for a technical document, the writer should consider the following questions:

- **Who is the material for?** Audiences that lack knowledge of or experience with the topic of the document may require more explanation and a simpler vocabulary than readers who are more familiar with the concepts.
- **What is the purpose of the material?** Decide if the information needs to define a problem, describe a situation, explain procedures, or persuade the reader to take a certain course of action.
- **How will the material be used?** A report that is used to support the decision to purchase a piece of equipment will contain different details than a step-by-step guide to using the equipment.
- **How will the material be published and distributed?** Whether the document will be published online, distributed as a computer file, or printed and bound can influence how the information should be presented.

- **Are there any format or length constraints?** The required length and style of a document may help determine what information and the level of detail that should be included.
- **When is the material due?** The objectives of a technical writing project should include finishing the document on time.
- **Who will approve the final document?** Know who is responsible for deciding whether or not the project is successful.
- **What is the budget?** How much money is available to complete the project?

ANALYZING THE AUDIENCE

should address the audience

primary: read and use it / need

The specifications for a technical writing project should address the probable readers of the final document. The intended audience of a document is a primary concern because the same information may be written different ways depending on the abilities and needs of the readers.

TYPES OF READERS

A document's readers can be divided into two categories: primary and secondary. The **primary audience** consists of the people who need the information and will use it to make decisions. The **secondary audience** includes any other people who later come in contact with the material. For example, a construction company may develop a safety plan to help superintendents make decisions about on-site procedures. The superintendents are the primary audience. The same company may be required to include a copy of the safety plan in a project bid package. The engineers and project managers who review the bid are the secondary audience.

A technical document should provide enough information to meet the decision-making needs of the primary audience. However, technical writers need to consider all of the readers who are likely to use the material.

When analyzing the audience of a document, a writer should research the likely readers' technical ability and current familiarity with the subject. Based on the audience's experience and knowledge, the writer chooses one of three strategies for presenting the material: highly technical, semitechnical, or nontechnical.

= writer

A **highly technical** presentation strategy is appropriate when the audience's background with the subject is similar to the writer's. Because the readers are probably familiar with many of the background concepts related to the document's topic, a highly technical document does not include basic exposition and interpretation. Writers of highly technical documents may use abbreviations common in the industry without defining them first. Graphs, charts, and equations may be included, but it is not necessary to interpret the raw data. Examples of highly technical documents include journal articles and reports for collaborators.

< writer

Semitechnical presentations are used when the anticipated audience is familiar with the topic, but has less experience, specialized training, or expertise with the subject than the writer. Semitechnical presentations may include definitions of technical terms, interpretations of raw data, and explanations of the conclusions. A laboratory manual written for a college class is an example of a semitechnical document.

A **nontechnical** presentation is targeted toward an audience that has little or no knowledge of or previous experience with the topic. When developing a nontechnical document, a writer should include enough information to help the reader understand the procedures, results, and conclusions without referring to outside references, but not so much that the reader becomes confused or bored. Whenever possible, technical terms should be replaced with simple language. Articles written for the popular media are examples of nontechnical documents.

IN · company

Technical documents may have different requirements depending on whether they are prepared for internal or external audiences. An **internal document** is one that is intended to be used only within the company or organization that prepared it. An **external document** is written for readers that do not work for the company that prepared the document. Internal and external documents may differ in how much background information is included, required formality, acceptable jargon, specific information provided, and format used.

outside company

When analyzing the audience for a document, a writer should research possible technical or accessibility issues. For example, some readers may not have Internet access on the worksite. Others may need visual instructions for completing a task. The document may need to be accessible to readers with a wide range of job descriptions, seniority levels, and reading abilities.

Technical writers should also analyze how the primary and secondary readers differ. If the primary and secondary audiences have significant differences in their understanding of the subject, requirements for the material, or technical proficiencies, then a technical writer may use one of the following strategies to meet the needs of both groups of readers:

- Prepare two or more versions of the document. Simply adding definitions of important technical terms, showing all steps of equations, or including explanations of conclusions can make a technical document more accessible to less knowledgeable readers.
- Include appendices that explain background material, interpret data, or explain conclusions for those readers who need additional information.
- Embed links in online documents. Popup windows with additional or background information are convenient ways for readers to get the explanations they need without navigating away from the document.

- Include a letter of explanation. Secondary readers may only need to refer to select portions of the document. A personalized memo listing the appropriate page or section numbers and providing any necessary background information can help the document meet the specialized needs of all readers.

RESEARCHING AUDIENCES

Audience research is important throughout the development cycle of a technical document. When planning a document, a writer may prepare a **technical brief** to help analyze the audience. A technical brief is a worksheet used to organize and summarize the likely readers' characteristics and needs. Once a draft of the document is available, representatives of the intended audience can review the document and give feedback about its readability and usefulness.

A technical writer has several options when researching the audience for a proposed document. Common methods of gathering information about readers include:

- **Focus Groups**
  A focus group of people similar to the intended audience of the document can be gathered and asked their opinions about what material the document should include and how the information should be presented.

  Focus groups may be online or in person. Members of the group are encouraged to communicate with each other. This interaction may bring up points that the writer had not considered. Focus groups can be an economical way of learning what an audience desires.

  The major disadvantage of a focus group is that the researcher may not be able to control the direction of the group members' conversation. In addition to veering off the subject, a focus group member may try to please the researcher or other participants and not give a complete and honest opinion.

  Focus groups are also vulnerable to observer bias. Researchers may only notice comments that support points that they already believe important.

- **Verbal Surveys**
  A technical writer may find out more about what the intended audience needs by asking potential readers specific short answer questions and recording the answers.

  Verbal surveys are efficient and can be used to study a wide variety of subjects. They are easy to administer and give data that can be analyzed statistically. During a verbal survey, researchers can control the topics discussed.

Because they are communicating directly with another person, verbal survey participants may not answer each question truthfully because of embarrassment or privacy concerns. The results of the survey may be skewed if groups of people choose not to participate. In addition, qualitative terms may have different meanings to each participant.

- **Written Questionnaires**
  Written questionnaires are used to ask short-answer questions. Because the questions are written instead of verbal, participants may feel more comfortable sharing honest responses. Because one-on-one contact is not necessary, written questionnaires can be quicker and cheaper to administer than verbal surveys.

- **Structured Interviews**
  Structured interviews are one-on-one research experiences in which each participant is asked the same questions in the same order. Structured interview questions are usually open-ended and designed to encourage participants to discuss their opinions.

Size + availability of audience

The most appropriate strategy for researching an audience depends on the size and availability of the audience pool, the time available for the research phase of the project, the amount of money available to complete the research, the type of questions the writer needs answered, and the kind of statistical analysis that the writer intends to perform on the results.

ENSURING THE VALIDITY OF DATA AND SOURCES

The references used in technical material are a primary factor in the accuracy and utility of the completed project. Including information from a poor source can reduce the audience's perceived validity of the entire document. Incomplete or inaccurate data can cause a reader to draw invalid conclusions.

When researching technical materials, writers can choose from a wide range of reference types. Possible source material includes:

highly technical

- **Periodicals:** Peer-reviewed journals include highly technical articles written by primary researchers. Magazines are more likely to have semitechnical or nontechnical articles.
- **Personal Experience:** Writers with extensive first-hand knowledge of the topic may draw on their own experience.
- **Experiments:** Researchers may use the results of documented and repeatable experiments as source material. Depending on the technical level of the document, the results may be summarized or included as raw data.

- **Lectures:** Direct quotes from lectures delivered by subject experts may be appropriate for semitechnical or nontechnical documents.
- **Websites:** A staggering amount of data is available on the Internet through university, government agency, business, nonprofit organization, and individual-supported websites.
- **Books:** Textbooks can help writers review concepts related to the document. Technical guides provide data about procedures and material properties.
- **Related Documents:** Previous versions of similar documents can be useful when writing in-house manuals, handbooks, instructions, and policies.
- **Interviews:** Personal interviews with experts can reveal information that is not available through other sources. Interviews can allow writers to clarify their understanding of concepts and verify the validity of their conclusions.

These references can be divided into two categories: primary and secondary sources. **Primary sources** offer firsthand experience with the subject. Primary resources include the writer's memory, researchers' observations, and interviews with experts. Primary resources also include the raw data recorded about experiments and transactions. **Secondary sources** include material that other people have drawn from primary sources. For example, books, literature reviews, laboratory reports, and magazine articles are secondary sources.

Not all references are appropriate as source material for technical documents. Potential references should be judged on the following criteria:

- **Relevancy:** Source material should be closely related to the topic of the technical writing project. Avoid using tangential information.
- **Reputation:** Certain experts, websites, journals, and reference books carry more weight in their respective fields. Whenever possible, choose standard sources over material that is not well known.
- **Reliability:** Before using a website as a source, find out who is supplying the information. Do not use research material that does not come from an organization or individual with verifiable and relevant credentials.
- **Bias:** Research possible conflicts of interest before relying on a source. Even highly credentialed writers may be biased toward a product, procedure, or philosophy.
- **Age:** Technical understanding and standards develop and change. Try to use the most current resources.
- **Verifiability:** Just because a statement is published in a book, article, or website does not mean that it is accurate. When researching a technical document, double-check source data. Verify conclusions with other sources.

A technical document crafted from inaccurate, dated, biased, or unreliable sources may discredit the writer and be of limited use to the reader. Finding, verifying, and using appropriate sources are critical steps in the technical writing process.

Purpose, Content, and Organizational Patterns of Common Types of Technical Documents

Technical documents may be divided into a few broad categories. These categories are based on the purpose, content, and organizational patterns of the document, but are independent of the industry or category for which the document was created. Categories of technical documents are reports, correspondence, manuals, and proposals.

REPORTS

Reports are written documents used to communicate an opinion or conclusion either internally or externally. Reports may be formal or informal.

Formal reports are usually extensively planned and researched. In addition to background information about the project or situation, they may include supplements such as glossaries and appendices.

Informal reports are prepared more rapidly than formal reports and are used when information must be shared quickly. They include little or no background information about the subject, require little research, and contain no supplements.

PROGRESS AND INSPECTION REPORTS

A progress or inspection report communicates details about a current project, including:

- What has been completed
- What problems have been identified
- What tasks still need to be finished
- What tasks are currently in progress

by workers   *by overseers*

Progress reports and inspection reports differ in the perspective of the writer. Progress reports are written by the organization working on the project. Inspection reports are written by the organization funding, commissioning, or overseeing the project.

Purposes of progress reports include:

- To reassure the client that the project is progressing
- To share information revealed in the course of the project
- To make sure the client and contractor understand each other's expectations for the project

Purposes of inspection reports include:

- To hold the contractor accountable to the schedule
- To make sure the contractor is meeting the terms of the contract
- To determine if the schedule needs to be revised

A progress or inspection report can be an informal or formal report. The type of report chosen depends on the type of reader, the size of the project, and the frequency of the reports. Informal reports are more appropriate for small projects, projects that are reported on frequently, or communications within an organization. Formal reports are more often used for large projects, projects with an infrequent reporting schedule, or reports that are intended for an external audience.

A formal progress or inspection report can be divided into an introduction, body, and conclusion. The introduction should summarize the purpose, objective, scope, personnel, clients and schedule of the project.

The body of the report should analyze the progress made on the project. During the analysis, the project can be divided based on three basic schemes:

- **Time:** The analysis can break the project into a daily, weekly, or monthly schedule.
- **Tasks:** The report can discuss the progress made based on component activities.
- **Topics:** The report can list the advances made in different categories of the project.

Following the body, the conclusion of the report should summarize the progress made on the project and emphasize any schedule changes or issues that are discussed in the body or the report. In a progress report, the conclusion can be used to reassure the reader that the project is advancing. In an inspection report, the conclusion can be used to reinforce in what ways the progress is satisfactory and in what areas there needs to be improvement.

FEASIBILITY REPORTS

Feasibility reports are used to communicate an opinion or recommendation about a possible solution to a problem. The report answers questions about the practicality of a proposed course of action or compares two or more possible solutions. A feasibility report may answer questions such as:

- Is there enough money in the budget to take the action?
- Is there technology available to support the action?
- Is there enough manpower to complete the action?
- Is there community or organizational support for the action?
- Are materials and tools available to perform the action?

- Does the action conflict with current regulations?
- Is the action likely to result in a successful solution to the problem or to improve the situation?

Formal feasibility reports are composed of the following elements:

- **Introduction:** The first section of the report should state the purpose of the document and provide an overview of the contents.
- **Technical Background:** The document should include any material the reader needs to understand the report's recommendations. Background information that is likely to be too elementary for the primary audience may be placed in an appendix.
- **Situation Background:** Details of the problem or situation for which the action is proposed should be included.
- **Requirements:** The document should include a list of criteria that will be used to test if the plan is feasible. The criteria may include characteristics such as cost, location, and time. The requirements should be defined according to one of three different strategies:
  - ✓ **Numerical:** The maximum or minimum quantity of the characteristic, such as maximum price or minimum speed.
  - ✓ **Yes/No:** Whether the characteristic exists or not, for example, "Is the lot zoned commercially?"
  - ✓ **Rating:** A qualitative value given by the writer or through an external entity, such as safety rating or aesthetic rating. The rating may be based on subcharacteristics which are numerical or yes/no.
- **Discussion:** The discussion section is used to describe the potential actions and explain how each meets or fails each requirement.
- **Comparison:** If more than one course of action is being studied, a comparison section is used to discuss the differences between the options. The comparison section may be organized as a whole-to-whole comparison or a part-to-part comparison.
  - ✓ **Whole-to-whole comparison:** The qualities of option A are discussed, then the qualities of option B. This process continues until all of the options have been examined.
  - ✓ **Part-to-part comparison:** The first requirement is discussed and each option's performance in that requirement is listed. The process is repeated with the second requirement and all subsequent requirements. For most situations, a part-to-part comparison scheme is more useful to the reader.
- **Conclusions:** The feasibility report may identify several conclusions. Types of conclusions include:
  - ✓ **Primary conclusions:** Simple conclusions about individual requirements. For example, "Option A is the cheapest."
  - ✓ **Secondary conclusions:** Conclusions drawn from balancing several primary conclusions. For example, "Although Option A is the cheapest, its low quality rating makes it unsuitable for this situation."

✓ **Final conclusions:** A final course of action decided on by considering all secondary conclusions.

The conclusion section summarizes the points raised in the comparison section and gives the reasons for the final conclusion.

- **Recommendations:** In the recommendation section, the writer explicitly states the recommended course of action and summarizes the reasons for choosing that option.

RESEARCH AND LABORATORY REPORTS

The purpose of a research or laboratory report is to educate the reader about a subject, to answer a question, or to solve a problem. Research and laboratory reports do not make direct recommendations about future decisions, although they may be used to support a proposal. They often take one of the following common forms:

- **Does X meet a specific need?**
    - Examples:
        - ✓ Does acupuncture relieve back pain?
        - ✓ Should the company hire an additional engineer?
        - ✓ Will the current storage facility be large enough for next year's crop?
- **Which will meet a need better, X or Y?**
    - Examples:
        - ✓ Which accounting firm should the company use?
        - ✓ Is acetaminophen or ibuprofen more effective at relieving muscle pain?
        - ✓ Which contractor will be the most economical choice for building the addition?
- **What causes X?**
    - Examples:
        - ✓ Why is statewide soybean production decreasing?
        - ✓ Why have product returns increased by 30% over the last quarter?
        - ✓ Why are more junior high school students choosing not to take advanced math classes?

The topic of a research or laboratory report should be narrow enough that it can be covered effectively without boring or overwhelming the intended audience.

When writing a research or laboratory report, it is important to cite the sources of all quotes, ideas, paraphrases, or graphical elements.

A research or laboratory report may begin with a short abstract that summarizes the question being researched, the methods used, the results obtained, and the conclusions drawn. The abstract should be one paragraph, with only one or two sentences used to summarize each topic.

The body of a research or laboratory report often begins with an analysis of the topic, question, or problem. There are two stages to an analysis. First, the subject is divided into small parts. Next, these parts are classified based on their similar characteristics.

The report then discusses the methods used to study the topic, answer the question, or solve the problem. In the case of a research paper, the methods may include gathering and reading other reports, interviewing experts, taking surveys, or observing situations. For a laboratory report, the methods section may involve explanations of experimental processes.

After the research methodology is described, the results of the research are revealed. The results may be presented in a table or text version. The format used depends on the type of data and the intended audience of the document.

In the conclusion section, the writer explains how the results relate to the main topic, question, or problem of the report.

CORRESPONDENCE

In order to function efficiently, members of an organization need to be able to communicate. Business communication may be between:

- Members of the same organization
- Members of different organizations
- Members of an organization and their clients
- Members of an organization and their customers
- Members of an organization and potential employees

Correspondence is written communication. Types of correspondence include memos, letters, manuals and proposals.

MEMOS

Memoranda, or "memos," are informal reports used to communicate information quickly within an organization and between members of different organizations. Memos seldom require extensive planning. They do not include background information or supplemental materials such as executive summaries or appendices. Memos can come in a variety of lengths and formats. They may be transmitted electronically in the form of e-mail, delivered by hand, or mailed.

Companies may have their own forms for memos or a standard form such as the one in Figure 1 may be used.

Figure 1: Standard Memorandum Form

MEMORANDUM

TO:
CC:
FROM:
DATE:
SUBJECT:
MESSAGE:

In some organizations, hardcopy or e-mailed memos are the preferred method for communicating information such as:

- **Research results:** The outcomes of surveys, tests, and reference searches that are conducted on a regular basis may be better communicated through memoranda than formal reports. For example, an engineer may need to review the data from daily concrete core samples at a construction site. Because the engineer does not need the background information and conclusion section that would be included in a formal report, a memo is sufficient.
- **Progress reports:** On large projects, regular progress reports can be used to communicate what tasks have been completed, what has been delayed, and where the project is ahead of schedule.
- **Schedules:** Agendas for meetings and trips may be better suited to a memo than a formal letter.
- **Proposals:** A memo may be appropriate to present an internal proposal. External proposals, those written for an intended audience that is not part of the writer's organization, may require a formal document.
- **Requests for Information (RFI):** Memos may be used for internal requests for information.
- **Meeting Minutes:** A summary of the events of a meeting may be sent to the participants of the meeting as a memorandum, unless the meeting was very formal or large.

Although more informal than letters, memos should still be written carefully. Because writers may be held legally responsible for the information dispersed by memos, they should include only accurate information and write with a professional tone.

LETTERS

Letters, although more weighty and formal than memos, should be more personal than reports. They may be written to inform the audience, to persuade the reader to take an action or form an opinion, or to request information.

Parts of a Letter

Although letters seldom use formal headings and subheadings, most can be divided into six parts:

- **Heading**
  The heading should include the return address of the sender in addition to the date the letter was written. Any elements that are included in the letterhead may be omitted from the heading. The left side of the heading is usually aligned at the center of the page.

- **Inside Address**
  The inside address includes the name, title, company, and address of the intended recipient. Whenever possible, a letter should be addressed to a specific reader. The inside address is aligned at the left hand margin of the document and positioned four to six lines below the heading.

- **Salutation**
  A salutation is a formal greeting used by the writer. The traditional salutation for business letters is "Dear" followed by the intended recipient's name. The salutation is two lines below the inside address.

- **Letter Text**
  The letter text contains the information or request that the writer is trying to communicate to the reader. The letter text is usually single-spaced with double-spacing between paragraphs. The letter text begins two lines below the salutation.
  The letter text can be divided into three parts:
  1. Introduction paragraph: The first paragraph of the letter text should identify the writer and the purpose of the letter. Introduction paragraphs should grab the reader's attention and encourage her to continue reading.
  2. Body: After the introduction paragraph, one or more paragraphs should be devoted to material that supports the purpose of the letter.
  3. Conclusion: The concluding paragraph unifies the introduction and body of the letter. It may offer more details or suggest a response.

- **Complimentary Closing**
  The complimentary closing of a letter is written two lines after the last line of the letter text. Traditional closings to business letters include "Sincerely," "Respectfully," and "Yours truly."

- **Signature**

  The signature section of a letter includes the writer's handwritten signature and the writer's typed name. The writer's name should be typed four lines below and aligned with the complimentary closing, with the handwritten signature between the closing and the typed signature. If applicable to the purpose of the letter, the writer's job title may be typed under and inline with the typed signature. If the letter is being written on behalf of a company, the company's name is written in full caps two lines below the complimentary closing. The writer's name is then typed four lines below the company name and the handwritten signature is added between the two.

- **Other Possible Elements**

  Letters may also include one or more of the following parts:

  - **Typist's initials:** If the letter is not physically typed by the person signing the document, the typist's initials should be placed two lines below the signature and aligned at the left margin. The typist's initials element has two parts. First, the writer's initials are written in capital letters, followed by a slash. Next, the typist's initials are written in lowercase letters.

  - **Enclosure notation:** If the letter is accompanied by a résumé, brochure, or other document, the number of enclosures should be noted just below the typist's initials. For a single enclosure, type "Enclosure." If multiple enclosures are included, type "Enclosures x" where x is the number of enclosures. For example, a letter that is part of a package of seven forms would be marked "Enclosures 7."

  - **Distribution notation:** Some letters may be sent to more than one recipient. If an exact copy of the letter is being transmitted to someone else, this information should be disclosed to the recipient. Not only is including a distribution notation a polite practice, but it can help streamline communication by minimizing redundant exchanges. The distribution notation should be added just below the enclosure notation. A distribution notation consists of the label "cc:" followed by a vertical list of recipients. For example:

    cc: John Smith
           Jane Clark
           Robert Jones

  - **Postscript:** A postscript may be added if there is information important to the reader that is not included in the letter text. If included, a postscript is added two lines below the last notation. A postscript should be aligned left and labeled with the abbreviation "P.S."

The placement of each element is shown in the sample letter shown in Figure 2.

Figure 2: Sample Business Letter

123 East Street
Shady Spring, WV 25918
January 10, 2008

David Jones, Project Manager
Smith Construction
765 Front Street
Upper Sandusky, OH 43351

Dear Mr. Jones:

I received your request to use the property in Springfield, Missouri as a staging and parking area for the adjacent construction site.

Although Reilly Enterprises owns the property, that lot is currently being leased to Courier Excavating for equipment storage. It is my understanding that Courier is not using the entire lot. If they are interested in subletting part of the land to Smith Construction, we would be willing to alter their contract to make this possible.

I have passed the information from your previous letter to Sarah Leonard, the owner of Courier Excavating. You can contact her directly at (123)456-7890.

If you need anymore information, please let me know.

Sincerely,

REILLY ENTERPRISES

Tara Spaulding

Tara Spaulding

TS/ab
Enclosures 3
cc: Sarah Leonard

P.S. We have other empty lots in the Springfield, Missouri area that may fit your needs. I have included a map with the available properties marked, a copy of our lease agreement, and a payment schedule.

Letter Forms

Some companies have their own preferred letter format. Others use the standard **semi-block** or **modified block** formats. Both semiblock and modified block letters have single-spaced letter texts with double-spacing between paragraphs. These forms differ in how the first line of each paragraph is treated. When writing a letter using a semi-block format, the first line of each paragraph is aligned left. In a modified block format, the first line of each paragraph is indented.

Types of Letters

Letters can be written for a variety of reasons. Most business letters can be classified as letters of inquiry, letters of complaint, letters of instruction, or job application letters. The type of a letter dictates the information included and the tone that should be used.

Letters of Inquiry

Letters of inquiry are requests for information about a service, product, person, policy, procedure, or organization. Letters of inquiry should disclose the purpose of the letter in the introduction paragraph or early in the letter text. The information needed should be described as specifically as possible.

Letters of Complaint

Letters of complaint are sent when the writer is dissatisfied with a product or service. Letters of this type should be directed to someone who is able to take direct action to relieve the writer's complaint. Letters of complaint should be written to communicate the reasons for dissatisfaction in a reasonable and objective way. The tone should be polite, but not apologetic.

Letters of Instruction

Letters of instruction are sent to help the reader understand a procedure. The directions should be complete, thorough, and clear. Time, material, and climate factors that may affect the outcome of the procedure should be mentioned.

Job Application Letters

An application or cover letter should accompany every résumé that a job seeker sends out to prospective employers. While a résumé lists the writer's accomplishments, education, and experience, the job application letter presents the image the writer wants to project. The purpose of an application letter is to secure a job interview.

Each job application letter should be personalized to the position for which the writer is inquiring. Application letters can be personalized by:

• Changing the inside address
• Using a specific name in the salutation

- Discussing experiences or areas of expertise that are related to the position
- Mentioning why the writer wants to work for the company, how the writer learned about the position, or why you are contacting the addressee.

RÉSUMÉS

A résumé is a list of a person's experiences, education, skills, and certifications. A résumé and an accompanying cover letter or letter of application may be sent by a job seeker to a potential employer.

Résumés can differ in format and content, but most contain the following types of information:

- **Contact Information**
  A résumé should include enough information that readers can use their preferred method of communication to respond to the writer. All contact information, including the writer's full name, street address, mailing address, telephone number, and e-mail address, should be grouped together at the top of the résumé.

- **Career Objectives**
  The writer's reason for sending the résumé should be stated after the contact information. The career objectives section should include what the writer wants from a job. This statement should be personal and show thought. It should mention both immediate and long-term goals. The first impression a potential employer forms about a job applicant may come from the objectives statement.

- **Work Experience**
  Applicants whose employment record is stronger than their educational background should list their work experience first. Applicants with a short or unimpressive work history may benefit from leading with their educational achievements. Wherever the work history section is placed, it should include the following information for each job listed:
  - Dates of employment
  - Name of employer
  - Type of employment (seasonal, contract, full time, part time)
  - Duties
  - Promotions
  - Increases in responsibility

Jobs should be listed chronologically, starting with the most recent.

- **Educational Background**

  Any special training or academic programs completed since high school should be included on a résumé. As in the work experience section, educational achievements are listed chronologically with the most recent listed first. A high school diploma should not be included unless it was part of specialized vocational training.

- **Other**

  The job applicant's hobbies, special skills, awards won, offices held, and volunteer work may also be included if the experiences were relevant to the job desired and present a good image of the applicant. Achievements that show leadership ability, organizational skills, or civic responsibility may be well suited to a résumé.

MANUALS

Manuals are technical documents that give readers the information they need to use, enjoy, understand, or maintain objects or situations. Manuals are written for consumers, technicians, and professionals. The tone used and details included depend on the knowledge and needs of the audience. A manual written for the owner of a particular car model would differ from one intended for the mechanics who will work on the machine.

Manuals often begin with a description of the object. A description may be subjective or objective. **Subjective descriptions** are based on opinion. They may be used to create an impression or mood. "The car is sleek and sporty" is a subjective description. **Objective descriptions** are based on facts, not opinions. "The car is a V-6 convertible" is an objective description.

Descriptions in manuals should be objective, precise, based on the writer's complete familiarity with the subject, and appropriately detailed for the intended audience.

Descriptive sequences are strategies for organizing the attributes of the subject. The descriptive sequence used in a manual may be spatial, chronological, or functional.

- **Spatial Descriptive Sequences**

  A spatial sequence answers basic questions about the visual condition of an object, such as:
    - What material was used to make the object?
    - What component pieces are involved?
    - What does the object look like?
    - How is the object positioned?
    - Are any parts especially prominent?

For most objects, there are several possible ways to organize a spatial sequence, including:

- Left to right
- Right to left
- Top to bottom
- Bottom to top
- Inside to outside
- Outside to inside
- Front to back
- Back to front

The direction used should reflect the way the intended audience needs to understand the object and the parts the writer wishes to highlight. For example, a camera with an advanced lens may be described front to back to emphasize the lens, while another model with a user-friendly interface may be described from back to front to call the reader's attention to the rear control panel.

- **Chronological Descriptive Sequences**
  A chronological sequence orders the parts of an object based on the assembly process used to manufacture the object. For example, when binding a book, the textblock is sewn and glued first. Next, the headbands and endbands are attached. Finally, the cover is fitted and fastened to the textblock. The chronological sequence of a book would follow the manufacturing process by describing the textblock, the headbands and endbands, and finally the cover.

- **Functional Descriptive Sequences**
  A functional sequence describes how the object works. The order is dictated by the functional sequence of the object itself. Each part is described in the order it is used. For example, a functional sequence of a digital camera could describe the user interface first, then the focusing element, lens, and storage capability. The final item in the descriptive sequence could be the process of removing and sharing images.

- **Combination Descriptive Sequences**
  In some situations, the most appropriate description for the audience of a manual uses a mixture of two or more sequences. A combination descriptive sequence can be used to make sure readers get the information that will be most useful and interesting without including extraneous material.

Even for the same object, distinct audiences may benefit from different descriptive sequences. For example, an owner's manual for a car may include a combination spatial/functional sequence. A mechanic who will be taking parts of the car apart and putting them back together may need a chronological sequence.

INSTRUCTIONS

Instructions are reader-oriented directions for doing a task or making an object. They should answer any questions the reader is likely to ask about the process and be detailed enough that the reader can complete the process without referencing other material. The technical level of a set of instructions is dictated by the knowledge and experience of the intended audience.

The introduction of an instructional document should:

- State the purpose of the instructions
- Define the process
- Identify the intended audience
- List the skills, knowledge, materials, and tools needed to complete the process
- Fill in any needed background information that the intended audience is likely to lack
- Define important terms used in the body of the instructions
- Highlight safety precautions

The body of a set of instructions should proceed through the steps of the process chronologically. The only exception to this is if there are important warnings or safety concerns. These should be clearly marked in a way that will highlight the warning to the reader and placed directly before the related step. If pullout warnings are overused, they may lose their impact to the reader. Instructional steps should be written in short, clear, and complete sentences. Each main step should be the topic of a new paragraph. The action voice makes most steps easier to understand. When possible, rework sentences in the passive voice to avoid using forms of the verb "to be." Table 1 compares examples of instructional steps written in both the passive and active voices.

Table 1: Comparing the Passive and Active Voices

Passive Voice	Active Voice
The solution should be measured.	Measure the solution.
The membrane is cut with the knife.	The knife cuts the membrane.
The reaction is contained by the hood.	The hood contains the reaction.
The results are recorded in the book by the technician.	The technician records the results in the book.
The excess liquid was evaporated by the increased heat.	The increased heat evaporated the excess liquid.

Using the imperative, rather than indicative, mood, increases the readability and emphasizes the action of the step. Instructions written in the imperative mood use an understood you as the subject. Table 2 shows how the tone of an instruction changes when it is rewritten in the imperative mood.

Table 2: Comparing the Indicative and Imperative Moods

Indicative Mood	Imperative Mood
You should be prepared for a volatile reaction.	Be prepared for a volatile reaction.
Before the water boils, you mix the two solutions.	Before the water boils, mix the two solutions.
You need to let the egg whites warm to room temperature.	Let the egg whites warm to room temperature.
You should not cut the grass too short.	Do not cut the grass too short.
Next, you mound the soil over the crown of the plant.	Next, mound the soil over the crown of the plant.

Transitional words and phrases between steps can help readers follow the sequence of the instructions and provide continuity throughout the document. Commonly used transitions include:

- First
- Next
- Then
- Afterwards
- While
- The next step
- Finally

Instructions can be confusing and difficult to follow if the structure, mood, or tone changes between the steps. The instructions on the left of Table 3 are written with inconsistent composition. In the right hand column, the same instructions are rewritten with parallel structure.

Table 3: Correcting Unparallel Structure

Parallel Structure

Unparallel Structure	Improved Instructions
When lining up for a road race, follow these guidelines: • Slower racers line up toward the back of the pack. • Unplug any electronics. • Running more than two abreast is considered rude • You should wait until the announcer gives the signal to go.	When lining up for a road race, follow these guidelines: • If you are a slower runner, line up toward the back of the pack. • Unplug any electronics. • Do not run more than two abreast as it is considered rude. • Wait until the announcer gives the signal to go.

Instructions written with parallel structure observe the following rules:

• The subject of each step should be the same.
• The verb tense of each step should be the same.
• The mood of each step should be the same.
• The tone of each step should be the same.

Instructions should end with a conclusion that summarizes the major steps of the process and emphasizes how the steps work together.

PROCEDURES

Instructions provide detailed steps for completing a process. **Policies** are rules that govern processes performed in a business, organization, school, or department. **Procedures** detail how policies are implemented.

Procedures may be updated in response to changing situations, for example:

• New tools and materials become available
• Safety concerns with the current procedures are noticed
• New processes are developed
• Internal or external policies change

Well-written procedures explicitly relate to a policy. The associated policy should be identified in the header or introduction of the procedure document.

Procedures should provide some benefit to the user, for example:

- **Ease:** The procedure may be designed to help the user complete his tasks easily or more efficiently.
- **Safety:** Following the procedure may help the user complete his work safely.
- **Acknowledgement:** The procedure may help ensure that workers are given credit for their input.
- **Security:** Following the procedure may give the user legal protection.

Procedures should be easy to understand and use. They should not be overly restrictive, but allow users as much freedom as possible while still following the associated policy. Use simple, concise, and clear language. Procedures should include instructions for completing any forms that are referenced.

Avoid using names, addresses, telephone numbers, or other details that are likely to change. Instead, use job titles and department names so that the procedures do not have to be updated if the staff changes or offices shift.

Companies and organizations may be legally responsible for their written procedures, so all facts should be double-checked. Businesses and organizations may use templates and style manuals to make procedures created by different technical writers appear cohesive. Elements commonly included in a written procedure include:

- **Header:** The title page or document header lists the origin and identifying information for the procedure, including:
    - ✓ The title of the procedure
    - ✓ The date the procedure was issued
    - ✓ The date the procedure will take effect
    - ✓ The office that approved the procedure
    - ✓ The office that issued the procedure
    - ✓ Any previously issued procedures that the current document supersedes

- **Overview:** The objectives of the procedure and the tasks for which the procedure should be used are often listed in the overview section.

- **Areas of Responsibility:** The scope of responsibility toward the procedure for each department, office, and job title should be listed. Areas of responsibility may include:
    - ✓ Who is required to use the procedure
    - ✓ Who can issue exemptions to the procedure
    - ✓ Who trains users to implement the procedure
    - ✓ Who enforces the implementation of the procedure

- **Procedure Body:** The body of the procedure gives the details of how to implement the policy. Terms that are likely to be unfamiliar to the reader, as well as words, phrases, and acronyms that are used only in the organization, office, or department should be defined. The body of the procedure can take many forms, depending on the organization or department requirements, the intended audience, and the policy that is being implemented. Possible forms include:
    - ✓ Checklists
    - ✓ Outlines
    - ✓ Paragraphs
    - ✓ Worksheets
    - ✓ Schedules
    - ✓ Flowcharts
    - ✓ Illustrations
    - ✓ Tables

- **References:** The reference section lists all policies, forms, manuals, and external regulations related to the procedure.

- **Help Information:** The job titles and offices that provide training programs, background information, tools, materials, or manuals that can help the reader carry out the procedure should be listed at the end of the document.

PROCESS DESCRIPTIONS

A process description explains the causes and effects of a process. This explanation may take the form of a narrative or an analysis.

- **Process Narrative**
  A process narrative describes the process from the writer's point of view. Written in the first person, a narrative emphasizes the writer's role in the process. Laboratory notes and police reports are often narratives.
- **Process Analysis**
  A process analysis is a subject-oriented description. This type of explanation breaks the process into a series of parts then categorizes and defines each part.

Both process narratives and process analyses should describe the process in a series of steps. The steps should be:

- **Chronological:** The description should begin with the earliest step in the procedure and continue explaining the steps in chronological order.
- **Logical:** Information should be given in the order that will be most useful for the audience. Readers should not have to jump from one part of the description to another to find the information they need.

- **Distinct:** Combining descriptions of steps can be confusing and frustrating to the reader.
- **Necessary:** Actions not directly related to the process being described should not be included.

Table 4 shows two narrative descriptions of the same process. The sequence and format of the original description makes the process difficult to understand. Information that is not necessary clutters the document. The revised description presents the steps in chronological order, follows a logical progression, separates each step, and only includes actions that are key steps to the process. The result is a more coherent and readable document.

Table 4: Example Process Descriptions

Original Description	Revised Description
When cooking the soufflé, I beat the egg whites until they formed firm peaks. I added a pinch of salt before beating to make this easier. I learned that trick from making meringue. Before beating the egg whites, I melted the cheese and mixed it with the milk and flour. I did this over medium-low heat with the small sauce pan that I like to use for steaming broccoli. I let this mixture cool for a while then stirred in the egg yolks. While this cooled even more, I beat the egg whites. The most important part of this step is to let the egg whites reach room temperature before beating them. Then I folded the egg whites into the cheese mixture. They took up a lot of room, so it was a good thing I had started with the yolks in a big bowl. Then I carefully poured the mixture into a casserole dish. The recipe called for a soufflé dish, but I did not have one so I used a casserole dish and it turned out fine. I baked it in a preheated oven at 350 degrees for 45 minutes.	First, I allowed the eggs to reach room temperature. Then I separated the egg yolks and egg whites each into large mixing bowls. While preheating the oven to 350 degrees, I heated the cheese in a small saucepan over medium-low heat. I added milk and flour to the cheese and removed the mixture from heat. I allowed the cheese mixture to cool for about five minutes then mixed it into the egg yolks. I added a pinch of salt to the egg whites and beat them until they formed firm peaks. I gently folded the egg whites into the cheese mixture and poured the mixture into a casserole dish. I baked the soufflé for 45 minutes at 350 degrees.

PROPOSALS

Proposals are written to convince the reader to take a certain action, such as hiring a company for a project or buying certain materials.

From the client's perspective, the proposal process consists of three phases. In the first phase, the client identifies a service or product that will solve a problem or improve operations. In the second phase, the client collects proposals of ways to satisfy the identified need. In the third phase, the client awards the job or contract based on the strength of the proposals.

Proposals can be classified by their origin, intended audience, and purpose. Proposals may originate as either solicited or unsolicited. Solicited proposals are sent at the request of a potential client. Unsolicited proposals are sent because a company or individual believes a potential client would benefit from using a service or product.

The intended audience for a proposal may be internal or external. Internal proposals are intended for use within an organization. External proposals are for readers in other organizations.

Proposals may be geared toward planning, research, or sales purposes. Planning proposals detail strategies for solving a problem or improving a situation. Research proposals seek approval or funding to research a problem or situation. Sales proposals try to convince potential clients to purchase a product or contract for a service.

Effective proposals are clearly written with a confident but polite tone. The underlying purpose of a good proposal is to convince the reader to grant money or approval, not to prove moral, technical, or intellectual superiority. Proposal writers should not insult or threaten readers.

SECTIONS OF A PROPOSAL

A proposal can be divided into three major sections: the introduction, body, and conclusion.

The problem is defined within the **introduction**, and a proposed solution is described. The introduction should briefly explain why the proposed solution is the best option. If the document is a sales proposal, the introduction should define why the company sponsoring the proposal is the most qualified to perform the proposed solution.

The introduction section may include some or all of the following subsections:

- **Objectives/Statement of Purpose:** The reason for writing the proposal and the outcome the writer desires.
- **Statement of Problem:** A description of the problem that needs to be solved.
- **Background:** Supporting information about the problem.
- **Need:** A description of the client's desired outcome.
- **Qualifications of Personnel:** A list of pertinent experience, education, and credentials of staff members who would be instrumental in performing the proposed solution.
- **Data Sources:** A description of methods that will be used to further investigate the problem if the proposed solution is implemented.
- **Limitations:** A list of any aspects of the identified problem that the proposed solution will not address.
- **Scope:** Delineates the contractor's and client's responsibilities in the project.

The **body** of the proposal fills in the details of the proposed solution established in the introduction. Subsections of the body may include:

- **Methods:** How the proposed solution will be achieved.
- **Timetable:** How long each phase of the proposed solution should take.
- **Materials and Equipment:** Specifications of supplies, tools, and equipment that will be used to implement the proposed solution.
- **Personnel:** Details of key people involved in implementing the proposed solution in addition to the number and job descriptions of crew members employed at each phase.
- **Available Facilities:** A list of the operating facilities that the contractor will supply.
- **Needed Facilities:** Description of facilities that will need to be obtained or made available by the client.
- **Cost:** Discussion of the breakout and total costs to the client of implementing the proposed solution.
- **Expected Results:** A realistic prediction of the outcome of the proposed solution.
- **Feasibility:** Examination of the likelihood of success if the proposed solution is adopted.

The **conclusion** of a proposal should include a summary and a formal request for action. The summary is a reiteration of the key points defined in the introduction and developed in the body of the proposal. The formal request for action directly asks the reader to take a specific step. The requested action may be to hire the contractor, contact a salesperson or project manager, update a work order, or purchase a product.

Elements of Technical Reports

Technical reports should be organized to best meet the needs of the intended audience. Elements may be included or left out according to the technical knowledge, reading level, time available, and information needs of the typical reader.

TITLES

The title of a technical report should be clear and tightly focused. Enough information should be included so that readers can make reasonable decisions regarding whether or not the report will meet their needs based only on the title. The title should use concrete and specific terms to describe the subject of the document.

Consider the following examples of titles for technical reports:

- Original: "Daffodils and Cornstarch"
  Revised: "The Effects of Cornstarch on Daffodil Germination"
  The original title is too vague to be useful to the reader. If two or more entities are listed in the title, the relationship between the entities that was studied should also be included.
- Original: "Smoother Drives Through Asphalt Additives"
  Revised: "Asphalt Additives Help Make Roads Smoother"
  The original title is ambiguous. Readers may not understand if asphalt additives will help them drive smoother or if they will learn about physically driving from one side of an asphalt additive to the other.
- Original: "Mergers Divide Parishes"
  Revised: "Parish Mergers Decrease Parishioner Involvement in Volunteer Ministries"
  The original title is confusing and unfocused. In the revised title, the cause and effects are specified.
- Original: "The Rate of *Ichthyophthirius multifiliis* Infections and Mortalities in the Common Goldfish Greatly Increases in Aquaria Where the Water pH is Below 4.0 or Above 8.2"
  Revised: "Aquaria pH Can Influence *Ichthyophthirius multifiliis* Infection and Mortality in the Common Goldfish"
  The title does not have to tell the reader the major details of the report. The revised title is more concise and removes the abstract adjective "greatly."

The purpose of a technical report is to communicate information to the reader. Because the title is often the first element of the report that the reader will see, it should set a tone of accuracy and completeness that will be continued through the rest of the report.

SUMMARIES AND ABSTRACTS

Summary statements are quick overviews of the document that come before the body of the report. After the title, the summary or abstract is usually the first section a reader sees. It must grab the audience's attention and encourage them to continue reading the document.

A summary statement should:

- Show an understanding of the reader's needs, problems, and philosophy.
- Clearly state the purpose of the document.
- Summarize the most important information from the body of the document.

The specific form of summary statement used in a report depends on the type and purpose of the document. **Executive summaries** are most often used in business proposals and reports. **Abstracts** are more common in scientific and research documents.

Summary statements include a one- to two-sentence synopsis of each main topic of the document. Executive summaries and abstracts include the following elements:

- Definition of the document's subject
- List of methods used to analyze the subject
- Results of the analysis
- Conclusions and recommendations
- Limitations of the analysis

Summary statements should be written as standalone documents. The audience should have a general understanding of the purpose, methods, results, and ramifications of the document after reading the summary statement.

Although the summary statement is one of the first elements of a technical document, it is usually one of the last sections written. Composing the abstract or executive summary last gives the technical writer the opportunity to solidify the structure of the document and identify the most important information. Examples of summary statements are listed in Table 5.

Table 5: Examples of Abstracts and Executive Summaries

Summary Type	Example
Executive Summary	The purpose of this business plan is to make a recommendation regarding Joe Miller's loan application. Joe Miller has applied for a $100,000 loan to purchase new equipment and renovate the building housing his business, Joe's Bar and Grill. Joe's Bar and Grill has been profitable for the last 5 years and fills a unique niche in the Worthington Area by focusing on the nontraditional student market. Joe Miller has a high credit rating and is offering the commercial property where Joe's Bar and Grill is located as collateral for the loan. Miller's income projections suggest that he will be able to repay the loan within 8 years. Based on the attached application, credit report, and financial records, I recommend First Community Bank approve Joe Miller's loan application.
Abstract	Salvador Construction Industries loses an average of $10,580 on each project because of concrete that does not meet specifications. To test the hypothesis that increased communication between the job site and the concrete batch plant would help ensure concrete be delivered at the job sites within the optimal pour period and reduce concrete wastage, the concrete suppliers at three job sites were sent hourly progress reports through e-mail throughout the pour process. Three projects running concurrently with the test projects served as controls with no additional scheduled communication between the job site and the batch plant. Concrete wastage at the test projects was 79% less than at the control projects. These results indicate that increased communication between the job site and the concrete suppliers seems to reduce concrete wastage.

HEADINGS

Section headings are used to increase the readability of a document by breaking up blocks of text and helping readers find the information they need without reading every word of the document. Word processing programs may have predefined section heading formats to help writers create document divisions quickly. These headings can later be used to create supplemental elements such as table of contents and indices.

Although section headings help readers to visually break long documents into manageable chunks, too many headings can interfere with the flow of the document. To decrease this interference, section structures should be both **cohesive** and **parallel**.

In a cohesive structure, all subheadings are related to the main heading under which they fall. A parallel structure is one where the each subheading under a single heading has the same relationship to the main heading.

The following heading structure is cohesive because each subheading is related to the main heading. However, it is not parallel. The first three subheadings list safety concerns but Subheading 4 introduces solutions to the safety issues.

Main Heading: Safety Issues at the Shady Point Construction Site
    Subheading 1: Outdated Equipment
    Subheading 2: Poor Safety Training
    Subheading 3: Ineffective Response Procedures
    Subheading 4: Proposed Solutions

This example structure can be rewritten to be both cohesive and parallel by upgrading the fourth subheading.

Main Heading 1: Safety Issues at the Shady Point Construction Site
    Subheading 1: Outdated Equipment
    Subheading 2: Poor Safety Training
    Subheading 3: Ineffective Response Procedures

Main Heading 2: Proposed Solutions

DEFINITIONS

The definitions section of a technical report is used to clarify highly specialized terms and concepts used in the report. If only terms with short definitions are used, they may be defined in the body of the report. However, if an important term requires more than one or two sentences for clarification, a formal definitions section can be used to call attention to the definition and to avoid interrupting the flow of the report text. When included, the definitions section occurs early in the report; often directly after the abstract or introduction.

The definitions section is not the place to define words and phrases that most of the audience will probably be familiar with. If the writer feels these terms need to be defined to make the report useful to a wider audience then the report should include a glossary. Information included in the definitions section may include:

- **Terms that are used different ways within the industry:** If a term has more than one commonly used definition within a field and the meaning of the term within the report is not clear from the context, the term should be defined in the definitions sections.
- **Terms with abstract definitions:** Some concepts are not concretely defined within a field. If a precise definition of a term is important to the methodology, discussion, or conclusion of the report, the definition used during the research should be stated. For example, social workers may disagree about what exactly constitutes psychological abuse. A report that studies the occurrence rate of psychological abuse among children in a geographic area should first define what is considered psychological abuse for the purposes of the study.
- **Job titles, locations, and names specific to an organization:** If a report intended for an external audience uses terms that only someone within the organization would understand, those terms should be defined. For example, researchers within a laboratory may understand where the "Rochester County Test Site" is located, but outsiders would not. If the location or description of the site is important to the data in the report and the report will be read externally, then it would be appropriate to include information about the site in the definitions section.

A definitions section differs from a glossary because the meanings listed in definitions section are only assumed to be valid within the scope of the document. A glossary entry may not give a complete definition of a term, but the definition is assumed to be valid inside and outside the scope of the document.

CONCLUSIONS

Some technical documents require writers to draw and describe conclusions based on the set of information drawn from references. The conclusion should address the most important aspects of the described problem or situation. A good conclusion relies on accurate data and reasoning.

Errors in logic can invalidate a document's conclusions. Some common logical fallacies that should be avoided in technical writing include:

- **Missing the point:** To miss the point is to draw a conclusion that is more extreme than the evidence supports.
- **Hasty generalizations:** A hasty generalization is a conclusion based on a sample size that is too small or limited.
- **Begging the question:** To "beg the question" means to base a conclusion on a piece of information that is essentially a restatement of the conclusion or to ignore flaws in a core piece of information.
- **Red herrings:** A red herring is a tangential issue that is addressed in order to distract the readers from the main problem.
- **Slippery slopes:** A slippery slope assumes a chain of events will happen, even though the evidence does not support the entire chain.
- **Weak analogies:** A weak analogy compares two things that are alike in some ways, but not in characteristics that are relevant to the discussion.
- **Appeals to authority:** An appeal to authority can take two forms: citing a person who is not an expert in the subject being discussed or failing to describe the reasons that support an expert's opinion.
- *Ad populum:* An *ad populum* ("to the people") argument relies on public opinion to support a position.
- *Ad hominem:* An *ad hominem* ("against the person") argument attacks a person who supports a dissenting position, rather than the position.
- *Tu quoque:* A *tu quoque* ("you too") attack points out the hypocrisy of a person who supports a dissenting position.
- *Post hoc:* A *post hoc* argument is one that assumes a causal relationship between two events.
- **Appeals to pity:** An appeal to pity is an attempt to get readers to accept conclusions based on sympathy.
- **Equivocation:** To equivocate is to use two meanings of a word interchangeably.
- **Appeals to ignorance:** An appeal to ignorance seeks to support a decision because a contrary decision can not be supported.
- **Strawmen:** Strawman arguments are built when a watered down or misrepresented version of one side is described and then attacked.
- **False dichotomies:** A false dichotomy is the mistaken view that there are only two possible solutions to a problem.

Examples of Logical Fallacies

Fallacy	Example
Missing the point	Students in the local private high school have a higher average on the ACTs than students at the public high school. Therefore, we should close the public high school.
Hasty generalizations	The last two trucks of concrete from that batch plant have had moisture problems. Therefore, all concrete from that plant has moisture problems.
Begging the question	All housing developments have drainage issues because drainage issues are an inherent part of designing a housing development.
Red herring	The first brand of albumin is the most economical choice for the laboratory because the manufacturer of the second brand supports an unpopular political cause.
Slippery slope	If the engineering department does not upgrade all computers within the next five months, employees will be unable to open documents from other departments and the company will be unable to complete existing engineering projects or begin new ones.
Weak analogy	Monkeys have an independent nature, just like cats. It is illegal to keep a monkey as a pet in this city; therefore it should be illegal to keep cats as pets.
Appeal to authority	We should relax regulations on the coal mining industry because Professor Howard says that the regulations are too extreme.
Ad populum	Most people in the office would prefer a different e-mail program, so it would be in the best interest of the company to switch.
Ad hominem	Rebar is not needed at the base of the structure. Mr. Bolen supports adding rebar, but his construction experience is limited.

Fallacy	Example
Tu quoque	Dr. Leeds has suggested tighter safety policies, but his department has been cited with more violations than any other.
Post hoc	The average weight of a newborn has increased since 1970. The number of Caesarean sections performed has also increased during that time. Therefore, larger birth weights cause more Caesarean sections.
Appeal to pity	The company should implement the changes proposed in this document because if these suggestions are not used, I will not get credit for my internship here.
Equivocation	The gene for blond hair is not as strongly expressed as the gene for brown hair. Therefore, brown hair is stronger and less prone to breakage than blond hair.
Appeal to ignorance	It has not been proven that user error had no role in the anomalous readings. Therefore, user error was a cause of the readings.
Strawman	People who do not vote to increase the school levy do not want to fund public services. Public services include the police force, water treatment plant, and garbage pickup. Without these services, residents' quality of life would suffer. Therefore, it is important to vote for the school levy increase.
False dichotomy	Parents must either stop allowing children to play video games or accept that reading scores on standardized tests are not going to improve.

Logical fallacies can be difficult to detect in complicated technical documents. Writers can reduce their logical errors by reviewing their conclusions with the following questions in mind:

- Are the cause-and-effect assumptions used to draw the conclusions valid?
- Are all arguments used to support the conclusions directly related to the conclusion?
- In drawing the conclusions, were a reasonable number of possibilities examined?
- Are the arguments used to support the conclusions factual?

If the conclusions presented in a document are based on invalid evidence or faulty logic then the document will be of limited use to the reader.

RECOMMENDATIONS

Recommendations are suggested actions based on the research results discussed in the report. A writer's recommendation may be one of the following:

- Accept one of the options described in the document
- Accept a combination of the options described in the document
- Reject all of the options described in the document
- Continue researching the situation

In addition to stating a suggested action, the recommendations should address the following questions:

- Does the recommended action solve the problem or answer the question?
- If the recommended action is taken, what parts of the problem or question would still need to be addressed?
- If the recommended action is taken, should it be modified from how it is described in the document?
- What immediate steps need to be taken to start implementing the recommended action?
- What answers still need to be answered before the recommended action is implemented?

The recommendations section should include a brief summary of the evidence used to choose the suggested action.

GRAPHICS

Visual elements can help readers understand a technical document, but if poorly used they can confuse and bore the audience.

Graphics in a technical document may include:

- Tables
- Illustrations
- Graphs
- Flow charts
- Schematics
- Photographs

Graphics should not be used lightly. Any visual element in a document should have a function. Possible uses of a graphic include:

- To call the reader's attention to a particular point
- To increase the reader's understanding of a set of information
- To summarize complicated information
- To show similarities between different data sets
- To show differences between different data sets

Any graphic in a technical document should be clearly labeled and discussed within the body of the report; otherwise the graphic should be placed in an appendix.
Graphics can be divided into two categories: tables and figures.

TABLES

Tables are lists of information arranged in columns and rows. They are used to summarize comparisons between categories of information. Each row and column of a table should be labeled to identify the kind of data listed and to define the units of measurements used. All items in a single column should use the same unit of measurement.

Tables should be numbered in the order they appear in the document. If footnotes are used within a table, they should be lowercase letters to differentiate them from the numeric footnotes used in the body of the document. Sources used to construct the table should be cited just below the table. The table and its associated citations should be set off from the body of the document with white space or a simple border.

The table below illustrates a simple table.

Table 6: Yearly Pea Production by Field

Year	Field 1 (pounds)	Field 2 (pounds)	Field 3 (pounds)
1999	86	72	95
2000	88	73	93
2001	32a	77	92
2002	92	72	102b
2003	89	76	132
2004	94	77	130
2005	99	72	127

[a] Field 1 was partially inaccessible due to flooding throughout growing period.
[b] Field 3 was treated with a proprietary fertilizer blend in late spring of 2002 and at the beginning of spring each subsequent year. No other field in the farm received the fertilizer.

Tables can contain numeric information, non-numeric information, or a combination of the two. Data categories can be simple or complicated. Table 7 shows how alignment, borders, white space, and shading can be used to help readers understand complex tables.

Table 7: Summary of Sales by Store and Year

	New Haven Location		Springfield Location		Weston Location	
Year	**2006**	**2007**	**2006**	**2007**	**2006**	**2007**
Units Sold	1898	1765	1628	1909	4576	3415
Revenue	$78,921	$75,452	$64,990	$80,060	$120,422	$102,444
Top Selling Item Number	XRT-178	CFT-459	RRY-652	XRT-178	XRT-178	CFT-459
% of Revenue	65.41	43.31	91.01	55.97	64.21	64.10

FIGURES

Any graphic that is not a table is considered a figure. Figures include charts, graphs, diagrams, and illustrations. Like tables, figures should be numbered according to the order they appear in the text. Tables and figures are usually numbered independently of each other.

Graphs

Graphs are visual representations of numeric information where the data is plotted on a coordinate system. **Bar graphs** are used to compare two or more data sets. On a bar graph, only one axis of the coordinate system needs to be numeric. The other axis can be qualitative, such as color, name, or flavor. In the bar graph in Figure 3, only the vertical (y) axis is numeric.

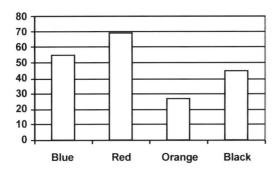

Figure 3: Average Points Scored by Team

In a **segmented bar graph** or **stacked bar graph**, the constituent parts of each category are shown. Figure 4 shows a segmented bar graph.

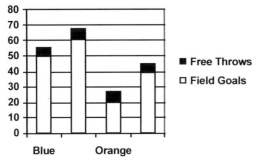

Figure 4: Average Points Scored by Team

In a **line graph**, both axes must be based on quantifiable measurements. Line graphs are used to show a change over time, distance, travel, size, or other measurable characteristic.

When constructing a line graph, it is important to keep the spacing on the axes consistent. Figure 5 shows a line graph with uneven spacing in the x-axis. The names of the months represent a measure of time. Because of the labeling in Figure 5, it appears that the time interval between January and March is equal to the interval between March and April and April or August. This causes a distorted graph. Figure 6 shows the same information with an even scale.

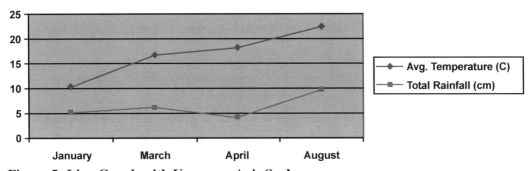

Figure 5: Line Graph with Uneven x-Axis Scale

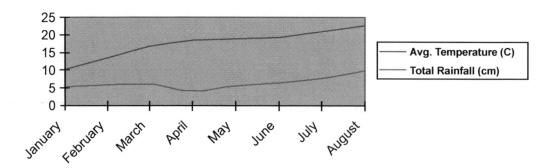

Figure 6: Line Graph with Even x-Axis Scale

No matter which form is used, a graph should include a descriptive title or caption. In segmented bar graphs and line graphs that include more than one line, the symbols used to differentiate data types should be defined in a legend. The legend should be placed in a visible place that does not interfere with a reader's ability to examine the graph.

The scales used in the axes should be adjusted to maximize the graph's readability while allowing the graph to fit on a single page whenever possible.

Bibliographic information related to the graph may be added just below the graph. Font size and formatting may be used to separate the bibliographic information from the body of the document.

Charts

Charts are graphic elements that show the relationship between two or more data types. Because charts illustrate the relative size or position of the data types, not the actual size, an axis is not needed.

Pie charts are charts that are divided into wedges. Each wedge represents a different category of information. The relative sizes of the segments are equal to the relative sizes of the data the wedges represent. Pie charts are most often used to show the percentage of component parts. The entire circle represents one hundred percent. The segments represent the percentage of the components. Figure 7 shows a pie chart.

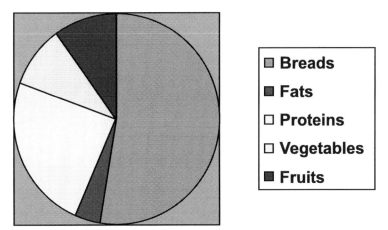

Figure 7: Breakdown of Average Daily Diet of West Elementary School Students

Pie charts are traditionally circular, but may be produced in a variety of shapes to match the subject of the chart or document.

Flowcharts are used to show the decisions involved in completing a process. Flow charts can be used to walk readers through a variety of procedures, from assembling a bookcase to mapping a sample of DNA. Readers that are confused by written instructions may find flowcharts easier to understand.

Organizational charts show the relative position of constituent parts. An organizational chart may be used to show how members or departments of an organization interact. Figure 9 shows a simple organizational chart.

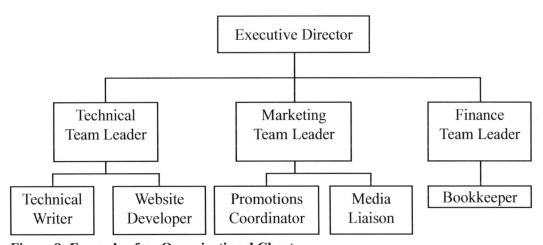

Figure 8: Example of an Organizational Chart

Diagrams

Diagrams are illustrations of items or processes. **Exploded diagrams** show the details of how parts of an object fit together. The component parts illustrated on an exploded diagram are shown slightly separated, as in Figure 9, so the reader can better understand which units are individual and which are already connected. Exploded diagrams may use simplified representations of the object. A key or legend can help readers identify each part.

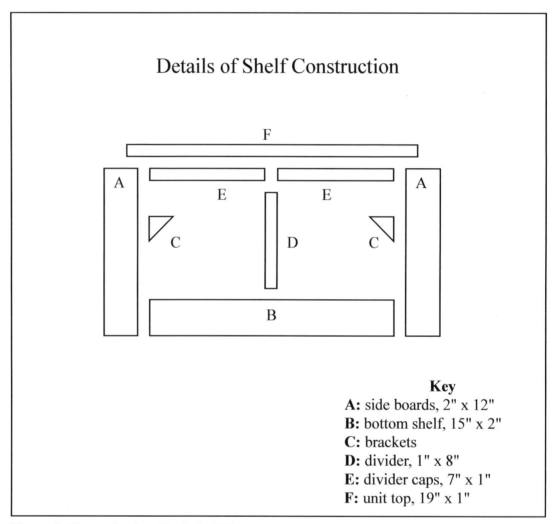

Details of Shelf Construction

Key
A: side boards, 2" x 12"
B: bottom shelf, 15" x 2"
C: brackets
D: divider, 1" x 8"
E: divider caps, 7" x 1"
F: unit top, 19" x 1"

Figure 9: Example of an Exploded Diagram

Two diagrams of a single item can vary drastically based on the angle from which the subject is drawn. For example, an exploded diagram of the front of a vacuum cleaner would look very different from an exploded diagram of the back of the machine. When using a diagram, a technical writer should choose the view that will be most effective in helping the audience understand the important information. The view used should be identified in the title or caption of the diagram.

REPORT SUPPLEMENTS

Reports may contain supplemental material that helps readers find the information they need or allows the report to be useful for readers with different technical or experiential background. Common supplemental elements include glossaries, footnotes, appendices, and indices.

GLOSSARIES

A glossary is a list of definitions of terms that are found in the document. Not all technical documents include glossaries, but when a glossary is used it should immediately follow the body of the document. A glossary is used to help readers understand specialized terms that might be unfamiliar. Because it does not interrupt the flow of the text, it can help make a document accessible and interesting to readers with a variety of technical backgrounds.

A glossary should only be included in a document if there are at least five terms that need to be defined. If less than five specialty terms are used, providing working definitions may be a better option. A **working definition** is a simplified description of a term. When a working definition is used in a technical document, it should be clearly stated when the term is first used and should be the only meaning of the term used throughout the document. When a glossary is used, it should be mentioned in the body of the document.

Terms that the primary or secondary audience is unlikely to understand and terms that are used in special or unusual ways in the document may be included in a glossary.

Any term included in the glossary should be clearly defined. The definition should identify the category the term falls within and list the characteristics that differentiate the term from the other members of the categories. For example, consider the following definition for the term "chair."

> **chair:** A chair is a piece of furniture that is intended to be sat upon. A chair has an attached back and is built to hold only one person at a time.

According to this simple definition, a chair falls in the same category as sofas and stools. They are all pieces of furniture that are intended to be sat upon. A chair is different from other members of this category because it has a back, unlike a stool, and is built to be occupied by only one person at a time, unlike a sofa.

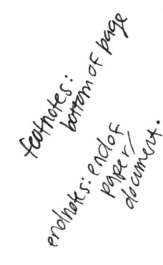

FOOTNOTES AND ENDNOTES

Footnotes and endnotes are used to give the bibliographic information of works cited in the body of a document. When using note style documentation, a number is written as a superscript after the information that is cited. If the paper uses footnotes, the numbers and the corresponding bibliographic entries for each page are listed four lines after the last line of text on the page. In endnote documentation, all of the notes are listed in a supplement to the paper. In both footnote and endnote notations, the citations are labeled chronologically according to how they appear in the text.

The form an endnote or footnote takes depends on the type of material being cited. Enough information should be included to allow the reader to find the source material if more information is needed. Table 8 shows note documentation styles for some common types of material.

Table 8: Examples of Footnotes

Description of Source Material	Example Citation Notes
Book written by one author	[1] Patricia Larkins Hicks, <u>Opportunities in Speech-Language Pathology Careers</u> (New York: McGraw Hill, 2007) 93. [2] Dorothy P. Dougherty, <u>Teach Me How to Say It Right</u> (Oakland: New Harbinger, 2005) 54.
Book written by two or more authors	[3] Froma P. Roth and Collen K. Worthington, <u>Treatment Resource Manual for Speech-Language Pathology</u> (Albany: Delmar, 2001) 201.
Edited book	[4] Lee Edward Travis, ed., <u>Handbook of Speech Pathology</u> (New York: Apple Century Crofts, 1957) 8.
Magazine Article	[5] Craig Boerner, "Sleep Levels in Children with ASD," <u>Advance for Speech-Language Pathologists and Audiologists</u> 17.49 (2007):14.

In some academic disciplines, parenthetical documentation is preferred over footnotes and endnotes for citing sources. In parenthetical documentation styles, the source is identified in the body of the paper. For example:

> A hyphen is used to form compound words such as great-uncle (Stoughton 150).

The in-text documentation refers the reader to the appropriate entry in the paper's bibliography. The citation includes the author or editor's last name and the page number from which the information was taken.

If the paper drew information from more than one work by the same author, the citation should include a key word from the title of the appropriate source. Just enough information is required to help the reader identify the right source.

In the following example, the citation sends the reader to page 85 of <u>Harbrace College Handbook</u> edited by John Hodges. Just enough information is included in the citation to allow the reader to find the correct entry in the bibliography or list of works cited.

> The past participle form of the verb *to spit* is *spat* (Hodges, <u>Handbook</u> 85).

When parenthetical documentation is used, the complete bibliographic information for each work cited should be included at the end of the paper.

Footnotes and endnotes may also be used to provide supplemental information about the material discussed in the body of the document. Common uses for background notes in technical documents include:

- Explanations for missing or anomalous data in graphs, tables, or charts
- Information tangential to the topic of the paper but of probable interest to the reader
- Minor details about methodology that might influence a process's repeatability.

The example in Figure 10 shows how footnotes can be used to provide background information in a technical document.

Figure 10: Using Background Footnotes

> We decided to use the test field at Cooper's Ridge after the soil tests at the other sites showed high alkalinity.[1] We divided the test field into eight sections and divided different concentrations of the herbicide to each section. The number of visible *Viola papilionacea* clusters and the average number of leaves from a random sampling of clusters at each site was measured 1, 2, 3, 4, and 6 days after application.[2]
>
> [1] Although current research suggests the pH of the soil would have little or no influence on the herbicide's effectiveness, at the time it seemed important to test the compound on a soil with a chemical composition as close to that found at the Glen Oaks subdivision as possible.
>
> [2] Measurements were not taken on the fifth day after herbicide application because a rock slide on the highway blocked access to the test field.

Notes used to give background information should not be mixed with notes used for source citations. Background and bibliographic notes may be distinguished by using numerical superscripts for one type and alphabetical superscripts for the other. Alternatively, background notes may be used with parenthetical source documentation.

APPENDICES

Appendices are used to supply more detailed information about material discussed in a document. An appendix may hold:

*   Formulas used to calculate data in tables or figures
*   Statistical analyses of data
*   Transcripts of interviews of lectures
*   Copies of forms, tests, or questionnaires
*   Tables and figures that are too large to be contained on one page
*   Maps
*   Photographs
*   Copies of laws, regulations, or letters
*   Raw data tables
*   Explanations of methods
*   Background information about theories needed to understand documents

Appendices should not be used to include needless information, details already covered elsewhere in the document, extremely basic material that the readers are likely to know, or figures or tables that are discussed in the body of the document (unless they cannot be sized to fit on one page).

Each major item should be in a separate appendix. Appendices should be titled clearly and labeled with consecutive capital letters, for example:

Appendix A: Raw Data from Buchanan County Soil Study
Appendix B: Raw Data from Holmes County Site Soil Study

Appendices should be mentioned in the body of the document when the related material is presented.

INDICES

An index is a list of the location of terms and topics within a document. The items in an index are arranged alphabetically by the term, with the page numbers of every occurrence of each term listed in numerical order.

If there are two or more qualifiers to a term then the qualifiers and the related page numbers are listed underneath in alphabetical order underneath the term, with the qualifiers indented.

If a term is discussed across several sequential pages, the entire range of pages is listed in the index.

Figure 11 shows an example index.

Figure 11: Example Index

Alchemy, 3-4

Art

          abstract, 14

          classical, 7, 9

          education and, 6, 8, 10, 19

          modern, 14-15

Bicycles, 32

Clocks, 1-3

          cuckoo, 1, 3

          mantel, 2

Clouds, 19-22

          classifications of, 19-20

          descriptions of, 21-22

Fire, 23

Jupiter, 7, 11, 13-18

Music, 9, 22

Although an index can be created manually, many word processing programs include tools to help automate the process.

Online documents may be made more useful by adding hyperlinks so readers can move directly from the index entry to the corresponding instance of the word or phrase.

PAGE DESIGN

The layouts used for a technical document may be influenced by some of the following goals:

- Increase the document's readability
- Call particular attention to certain information
- Establish the writer or publisher's credibility
- Adhere to the client's requirements
- Help the document stand out among similar publications

FORMATTING ON PAPER

The **format** of a document refers to how the text and graphics are arranged on the page. Formatting elements include:

- Typeface
- Alignment
- Spacing

Typeface refers to the shape of the letters used in the text of the document. The typeface chosen for a document will affect the readability of the text and help set the character of the document.

Letter types are categorized by the following characteristics:

- **x-height:** the height of a lowercase x, which reflects the height of the main bodies of the lowercase letters
- **cap height:** the height of the uppercase letters
- **ascender:** the height of the segment of lowercase letters such as h, d, f, and b that rises above the x-height
- **descender:** the height of lowercase letters such as p, j, y, and q that falls below the baseline
- **bowl:** the empty space inside letters such as Q, O, and D.
- **serif:** decorative strokes at the top and bottom of letters

These characteristics are used to divide typefaces into four main groups. Conventional types use serifs and have small x-heights. Dignified types have serifs and large x-heights. Modern types also have large x-heights but do not use serifs. Specialty types are exaggerated letter forms.

The **alignment** of a line of text refers to the physical placement of that line on the paper. Text alignment may be:

- justified, or flush, on both the left and right margins
- flush on the left margin and ragged on the right margin
- ragged on the left margin and flush on the right margin
- centered on the page

Spacing refers to the room between letters, words, lines, and paragraphs. The default settings for word processing applications leave roughly 120% of the type size for each line of text. Decreasing this spacing tends to make the text less readable, but will allow more text to fit on a page. Less line space can also help black text look more cohesive. Any page of a document can be divided into three spaces. **Gray spaces** are areas that are occupied by text. **Black spaces** hold graphics. **White spaces** are areas without text or graphics. Black space tends to attract the reader's attention. Gray space contains the main information of the document. White space helps break up the gray and black spaces, allowing the reader's eyes to rest and making the document easier to read.

The arrangement of black, gray, and white space can be used to group, separate, and emphasize information in the document. Some common ways of using different spaces include:

- **sinks (drops):** bands of white space at the top of the pages
- **vertical white spaces:** bands of white space to the side of the text
- **borders:** rectangular black space used to separate the body of the document from the margins
- **rules:** lines used to separate an element from the rest of the page
- **boxes:** rectangles used to frame a single, supplemental element from the rest of the page
- **bleeds:** a graphic that flows to the end of the paper

FORMATTING ONLINE

Some technical documents are created to be viewed on a computer screen. Electronic documents face challenges distinct from documents that will be published on paper, including:

- Reading long blocks of text on a computer screen can be fatiguing because of how light is projected from the monitor and the contrast between the foreground and background.
- Because only a limited amount of text is visible at once, readers may have to scroll vertically and horizontally to access the information.
- Readers may use different browsers, display options, and hardware. Some readers may decide to print out the material and read the hardcopy. Electronic documents must have versatile and flexible formats.

The following guidelines can help maximize an electronic document's readability and ease of use:

- Use only one column to minimize the need to scroll up and down the screen.
- Maximize the white space by using large margins and paragraph spacing.
- Break the test into visual blocks by using subheadings.
- Connect supplemental material to the body of the document through hyperlinks.
- Choose typefaces that are easy to read on the screen and are available on most computers.
- Keep backgrounds simple.

When distributing an electronic document, choose a file format that will make accessing the document and using the information easy for the audience. The three most common formats used to save and distribute technical documents are text files, HTML, and portable document format (pdf).

Text files can be created directly from and opened by word processing applications. A major advantage of text files is that most computer users have access to a word processing program and will be able to open the file. However, this also means that readers will be able to edit the information in the document and change the formatting. If an altered document is distributed to other readers, the changes may be attributed to the original writer of the document. Text files can become too large to send by e-mail if they contain many graphic or format elements.

HTML files tend to be small. HTML files support hyperlinks and can be opened by most computer users. A disadvantage of publishing a document as an HTML file is that there are limited formatting options. If a reader chooses to print an HTML file, the hardcopy may not look the same as the on-screen version.

Both text and HTML files may appear differently if the typeface used to create the document is not available to a reader. An advantage to publishing the document as a pdf is that the fonts are embedded in the file, so the reader sees the document as the writer intended. If a reader chooses to print the document, the hardcopy will be formatted as it appeared on the screen. Software to open pdf files is freely available; however, special applications are needed to create the files.

 Technical Editing

An effective technical document provides information the reader needs in a form that is clear and accessible. Before publication and distribution, a document should be edited to make sure each sentence conveys the material accurately, supports the image the writer desires, and is easy to understand.

CLARITY

Clear writing is unambiguous. Each sentence in a document should have only one possible meaning. Readers should not have to look for context clues to determine what the writer meant. Table 9 shows how ambiguous sentences can be rewritten for clarity.

Table 9: Ambiguous and Unambiguous Writing

Ambiguous	Unambiguous
Everyone was touched by the singer.	Everyone was touched by the singer's voice.
The titer can be achieved by three processes.	The titer can be achieved by any one of three processes.
We could not recommend a better method.	We recommend using this method.

Writing in the negative can make sentences wordy and unclear. Rewriting the sentences to remove negative words such as "no," "not," and "none" can sometimes make sentences shorter and easier to understand, as the examples in Table 10 show.

Table 10: Rewriting Negative Sentences

Original Sentence	Rewritten Sentence
We did not expect the budget to stay the same this quarter.	We expected the budget to change this quarter.
The samples were not treated the same.	The samples were treated differently.
It will not be possible to start this job on time.	Starting this job on time is impossible.
None of our engineers were able to solve this problem.	Our engineers were unable to solve this problem.

COMPLETENESS

Completeness refers to the level of detail included in a document. Not all details require the same amount of completeness. For example, a process description of a laboratory technique included as a sidebar of a magazine article may not need to be as complete as a description of the same process in a reference handbook for researchers. In the magazine version, the purpose of the description is to familiarize the reader with the theory behind the technique. On the other hand, researchers who use the reference handbook version will need to know how much of each reagent to add, reaction times, and required conditions.

The desired level of completeness of a document depends on:

- **The knowledge level of the writer:** Writers should never attempt to include more details about a subject than they thoroughly understand and are able to verify.
- **The needs of the audience:** Including too many details can confuse and intimidate readers, but a document that is incomplete with regards to the readers' needs may not be useful.
- **The size constraints of the document:** If a document needs to be less than a certain size, then details can be prioritized and low priority details may necessarily be left out.

Of these factors, the needs of the audience should take precedence. If the writer is not knowledgeable enough about the subject to include the appropriate level of detail, additional research is required.

ACCESSIBILITY

Accessibility refers to the degree to which a document can be used by readers. Technical documents should be accessible to the intended audience. The vocabulary, sentence structure, and page layout should be sophisticated enough to appeal to the reader without being overly technical or intimidating.

VOCABULARY

The vocabulary used in a technical document should be selected after considering the reading level, technical expertise, and experience of the audience. Technical writers should not use any term that they are not able to define.

Regional, archaic, and nonstandard terms should be avoided in technical documents. **Regional terms** are words and phrases that are not generally used outside of a geographic area. **Archaic terms** are words and phrases that are not generally used in modern communication but were common in previous decades. **Nonstandard terms** are words, phrases, and usages that are widely used in informal communications but are out of place in formal documents.

Jargon is specialized language used in a field of study or profession. Jargon may be appropriate in a document written for a highly technical audience, but it should be avoided when it is unnecessary or when the reader may be unfamiliar with the terms.

Sexist language is not appropriate in technical documents. Sexist language includes:

- Referring to both men and women with the generic term "man."
- Feminizing words that do not denote gender—for example, "male secretary," "female surgeon," "authoress."
- Assuming someone is male or female based on his or her profession, hobbies, preferences, or actions.

Strategies for avoiding sexist language in technical documents include:

- Rewriting sentences to avoid using pronouns
- Rewriting sentences to use a plural pronoun instead of a singular pronoun
- Alternating masculine and feminine singular pronouns throughout the document
- Using a combined masculine and feminine singular pronoun such as "his/her," or "he or she."
- Using gender-neutral labels

Table 11 shows some ways sexist language can be rewritten to be more appropriate for technical documents.

Table 11: Revising Sexist Language

Original	Revised	Revision Strategy
I will contact your secretary about the changes. She should have the papers ready before noon.	I will contact your secretary about the changes. The papers need to be ready before noon.	Rewrote sentence to avoid pronoun
We would like to hire an entry-level civil engineer. He should have passed the EIT exam and graduated in the top quarter of his class.	We would like to hire an entry-level civil engineer. Qualified applicants will have passed the EIT exam and graduated in the top quarter of their class.	Rewrote sentence to use plural pronoun

| All policemen should report to the conference room after their shifts. | All police officers should report to the conference room after their shifts. | Used gender-neutral label |
| All attendees and their wives are invited to attend the social after the conference. | All attendees and their spouses are invited to attend the social after the conference. | Used gender-neutral label |

SENTENCE STRUCTURE

Readers are more engaged by paragraphs composed of a variety of sentence structures and lengths. Combining different sentence forms makes technical documents more interesting and accessible.

Sentences are classified by their composition of independent and subordinate clauses. A clause is a group of words within a sentence that contains a subject and a predicate. An **independent clause** is a clause that can stand alone as a sentence if punctuation is added. A **subordinate clause** is a clause where the predicate begins with a subordinate conjunction or relative pronoun. Some subordinate conjunctions and relative pronouns are listed in Table 12.

Table 12: Commonly Use Subordinate Conjunctions and Relative Pronouns

after	although	As soon as	as if	as though
because	before	even if	even though	how
if	now that	once	provided	provided that
since	so that	that	though	till
unless	until	what	when	whenever
where	wherever	whether	which	while
who	whoever	whom	whose	why

Table 13 lists some examples of independent and subordinate clauses.

Table 13: Examples of Independent and Subordinate Clauses

Sentence: After the fish were tagged, they were released back into the stream.	
Independent clause:	they were released back into the stream
Subordinate clause:	after the fish were tagged
Sentence: The dog was detained and the suspect was chased while the detectives inspected the area.	
Independent clauses:	the dog was detained the suspect was chased
Subordinate clause:	while the detectives inspected the area
Sentence: We sealed off the area and tested the soil for lead.	
Independent clauses:	we sealed off the area we tested the soil for lead
Subordinate clause:	None

A **simple sentence** has only one independent clause. For example:

- ✓ The test was negative.
- ✓ Our company was unable to meet the demands.
- ✓ The chemical spill was contained.

A **compound sentence** contains two or more independent clauses. In other words, two or more simple sentences combined with commas and a coordinating conjunction make a compound sentence. For example:

- ✓ The samples were contaminated and we were unable to use them.
- ✓ The proposal letter addresses the problem, suggests a solution, and gives relevant contact information.
- ✓ The concrete was too wet, the outside temperature was too cold, and the aggregate was too small.

Complex sentences consist of one independent clause and one or more subordinate clauses.

- ✓ Unless we find another contractor, the project will have to be canceled.
- ✓ Although I contacted the human resources department, they were unable to fill the position.
- ✓ Now that the data has been interpreted, we are able to write the conclusions.

A **compound-complex** sentence is formed by at least one subordinate clause and two or more independent clauses. For example:

- ✓ After we demolished the structure, we surveyed the site and the engineers began designing the new building.
- ✓ We had enough samples to make the experiment statistically valid and we were able to continue the study, even though the accident destroyed some of the slides.
- ✓ The project funding should clear tomorrow and be in the account by Thursday, provided the foundation releases the money today.

The original paragraph in Table 14 is composed only of simple sentences. The revised version uses a variety of sentence structures and lengths to make the passage less boring and more readable.

Table 14: Sentence Variety in Paragraph Accessibility

Original	Revised
An ELISA is a laboratory procedure. It is used to test for the presence of a particular antibody. It is a routine procedure in our microbiology laboratory. Some ELISA protocols yield visible results. Other protocols require a digital reader.	An ELISA is a laboratory procedure routinely used in our microbiology laboratory to test for the presence of a particular antibody. Although some ELISA protocols yield visible results, others require a digital reader.

PAGE LAYOUT

The arrangement of text, figures, and tables on the page must balance attractiveness and space constraints with reader accessibility needs. Strategies for making a page more accessible to the audience include:

- Increasing the size of the type
- Adding white space between text and graphic elements

- Increasing margins
- Using a serif typeface for the body of the document
- Incorporating clear headings and subheadings
- Limiting the number of typeface used on the page
- Emphasizing key words or ideas by using bold or colored type
- Aligning the text to the left margin
- Leaving the right margin ragged
- Reducing the number of columns

Not all of these strategies are appropriate in every situation. For example, a document that needs to fit long and detailed instructions into a small space may need to reduce the size of the typeface. For a publication that requires formality more than wide reader accessibility, a three- or four-column layout with aligned right margins may be desirable. Documents that will be published online have different accessibility considerations. Most people read slower from a computer screen than they do from paper, so online documents should have shorter sentences with simple structures.

Because reading from a monitor can be fatiguing, paragraphs should be limited to two or three sentences. Headings and subheadings are important features for online documents because they encourage readers to skim the text and find the information they need. Readers may find it easier to skim when paragraphs are ordered so that the topic or conclusion sentence is first.

Left-aligned text is much easier to read onscreen than justified, centered, or right-aligned text. Text that is not left-aligned forces the viewer to read more slowly. Although these formats can be used to emphasize safety warnings or other important notes, reading justified, centered, or right-aligned text for a long period of time can cause fatigue and frustration.

Bulleted and numbered lists can help make online and in-print documents more accessible. Lists are less intimidating than long blocks of text and give the audience a break from reading material horizontally. Because readers' attention is drawn to lists, lists can be used to emphasize important material.

CONCISENESS

Technical documents should be tightly written. Readers of reports, letters, memos, and manuals need to be able to get the information they need quickly. They may lose patience if they need to wade through pointless or redundant material.

Concise writing is less likely to be misunderstood. Consider the following excerpt from a proposal letter:

> I would like to mention that we are not going to be able to start on the project in the time frame that is stated in your bid package. As we discussed through e-mail with your head engineer, we would be more than happy to get started working on the project just as soon as we can.

A reader who is rushed may overlook the important "not" in the first sentence and miss the main idea of the cluttered paragraph. A simpler and briefer version of the excerpt would reduce the chance of misunderstanding.

> We are unable to meet the time frame defined in your bid package.

Avoid using unnecessary words and phrases. Some commonly used prefaces that seldom add meaning to a sentence include:

- "Actually"
- "Without further ado"
- "The important part of this is"
- "The reason for sending this letter is that"
- "What I need to know is"
- "All things considered"

Sentences with superfluous phrases should be rewritten for conciseness, as shown in the Table 15.

Table 15: Editing for Conciseness

Original Sentence	Rewritten Sentence
The reason for sending this letter is that we are requesting a progress payment for the Utah Street project.	We are requesting a progress payment for the Utah Street project.
The important part of this is that we are ahead of schedule and will begin pouring concrete next week.	We are ahead of schedule and will begin pouring concrete next week.
Actually, we have already prepared the site for the pour.	We have already prepared the site for the pour.
What I need to know is when can we expect payment for the work that is already completed?	When can we expect payment for the work that is already completed?

The use of certain words and phrases should be minimized in technical documents to keep the writing concise. Rewrite to avoid overusing:

- "of"

  Original: "These are the samples of the blood from the patients."
  Revised: "These are the patients' blood samples."
  Original: "I will send the report of the demolition."
  Revised: "I will send the demolition report."

- "to be"

  Original: "The concrete is thought to be acceptable."
  Revised: "The concrete is thought acceptable."
  Original: "The design is not as good as we wanted it to be."
  Revised: "The design is not as good as we wanted."

- "that"

  Original: "The sample that the technician drew was contaminated."
  Revised: "The sample the technician drew was contaminated."
  Original: "We always knew that this job could be successful."
  Revised: "We always knew this job could be successful."

- "which"

  Original: "The bridge which we designed last fall will be built next year."
  Revised: "The bridge we designed last fall will be built next year."
  Original: "That was not which one I would have selected."
  Revised: "That was not the one I would have selected."

Trite statements seldom add more than clutter to a technical document. Leave out clichés or rewrite them in more concise forms, as in Table 16.

Table 16: Avoiding Trite Phrases

Original Sentence	Rewritten Sentence
We seek to employ the best and brightest candidates.	We are looking for qualified candidates.
With this network configuration, your employees will be zooming down the information superhighway.	This network configuration offers fast Internet connectivity.
Installing this software is a no-brainer.	Installing this software is simple.

We would like this project, now the ball is in your court.	We hope to hear from you soon.
Our hardware is high-tech and state of the art.	We recently updated our hardware.

CORRECTNESS

The usefulness of a technical document can be limited by inaccurate language. Language used in reports, manuals, or correspondences should be exact, specific, and concrete.

Exaggerations and overstatements should not be included in technical documents. Writers should not assume that a reader will be able to differentiate between factual statements and claims that are inflated for artistic affect.

Technical writers should be careful when including claims that a product or service will be the best or most attractive. Even if anecdotal evidence is available to support the claim, there is no guarantee that every reader will have the same experience. Claims that cannot be backed up with solid evidence should be rewritten.

Table 17 shows how exaggerations can be revised to be more appropriate for technical documents.

Table 17: Revising Overstatements and Exaggerations

Original Sentence	Revised Sentence
This stereo will fill any room with the most wonderful music you have ever heard.	Ninety percent of the survey participants rated the performance of the stereo as "excellent" or "superior."
Unless the board takes the steps recommended in this report, the school system will be broken down past the point of repair within ten years.	If the current budget trend continues, the school system will be operating at a deficit within ten years.
The absolute best albumin comes from the Lifeline Science Supply Company.	Our laboratory has found the albumin from the Lifeline Science Supply Company is consistently good.

A generalization is a form of exaggeration where a characteristic of a few members of a group is used to describe the entire group. Generalizations should be rewritten to protect the document's correctness, as in the examples in Table 18.

Table 18: Revising Generalizations

Original Sentence	Revised Sentence
Any intern could live comfortably on that stipend.	The internship stipend is valued 20% above the national average for schools of comparable size.
None of the engineering graduates will have to worry about finding a job.	More companies are recruiting engineering graduates this year.
No one needs 5000 psi concrete.	Only highly specialized structures required 5000 psi concrete.

Sarcasm and humor are not appropriate in technical documents. Sarcastic language is unprofessional, and there is a risk that a reader may not understand that a statement was not meant to be taken literally. Euphemisms should also be avoided in technical writing. Any function, item, or situation that needs to be included in a document should be referred to by its name, title, or description.

Flowery language does not belong in technical documents. Because abstract phrases may mean different things to different readers, they can only add confusion to a manual, report, or correspondence. Any description used in a technical document should be as accurate as possible and as specific as needed for the purpose of the document.

Terms that are used incorrectly can confuse readers. Writers should be careful to choose words that accurately convey the required meaning.

SEQUENCE

Arrangement can influence what points the reader notices and the overall usability of the document. Sequence can be considered on the sentence level, paragraph level, and document level.

SENTENCE-LEVEL SEQUENCE

Readers tend to focus on the words that appear at the beginning and at the end of a sentence. Writers can take advantage of this inclination by moving important words away from the middle of sentences.

Consider the following excerpt from a client's letter to a contractor:

> We need to know what you are going to do about the problem with the sub-contractors at the St. Paul's site.

The sentence can be rearranged to emphasize the word "problem."

> We need to know what you are going to do about the St. Paul's site subcontractor problem.

To add even more emphasis, "problem" can be moved to the front of the sentence.

> About the problem with the subcontractors at the St. Paul's site – we need to know what you are going to do.

Sentences can be made more forceful if they are reordered to avoid beginning with "There are" or "There is."

- Original: "There is a danger associated with inhaling the gas."
  Revised: "Inhaling the gas is dangerous."
- Original: "There are many reasons for the stock's poor performance."
  Revised: "The stock performed poorly for many reasons."

PARAGRAPH-LEVEL SEQUENCE

The main idea should not be buried in the middle or end of a paragraph. Readers should be able to skim the first line or two or a paragraph and determine if they need to continue reading the supporting sentences or if they should look elsewhere for the information they need.

In the example paragraphs from Table 19, the most important idea is that clothing designers may have limited labeling and advertising rights if they choose to use trademarked fabrics. In the original paragraph, this idea is not stated until the third sentence. A reader may skim the first sentence and assume the paragraph will explore ways large chemical methods create images for their technical fibers. The revised paragraph states the main idea in the first sentence. This sequence emphasizes the purpose of the paragraph and improves the usability of the document by making it easier for readers to find the information they need.

Table 19: Paragraph-Level Sequencing

Original	Revised
Large chemical companies may spend millions of dollars creating an image for their technical fabrics. In order to protect the image, they may define how the fabric can be used or marketed by clothing manufacturers. Designers who use trademarked fabrics may not be able to label or advertise their creations freely. For example, athletes that are part of a marketing campaign for one technical fabric may not be able to appear in advertisements for clothing made of a similar fabric produced by a different company.	Designers who use trademarked fabrics may not be able to label or advertise their creations freely. Large chemical companies may spend millions of dollars creating an image for their technical fabrics. In order to protect the image, they may define how the fabrics can be used or marketed by clothing manufacturers. For example, athletes that are part of a marketing campaign for one technical fabric may not be able to appear in advertisements for clothing made of a similar fabric produced by a different company.

DOCUMENT-LEVEL SEQUENCE

The most effective sequence structure for a document depends on the writer's purpose. When the document is intended to persuade the reader to agree with the writer's conclusion, the strongest evidence to support the conclusion should be presented first. Data that supports the key piece of research should follow. Data that the writer wishes to de-emphasize should be placed in the middle of the body of the document, not at the end. If the document is intended to instruct the reader about a subject or process, the sequence should follow the most logical progression for examining the topic. This is most often a chronological, functional, or spatial descriptive strategy.

A document written to solve a problem or answer a question usually starts by analyzing the problem or question using a chronological, functional, or spatial sequence. After the analysis, the benefits of the answer or problem are then discussed within the same sequence framework used to analyze the problem.

UNITY

Unity refers to the extent to which the elements of a document develop a shared idea. A technical publication's unity can be evaluated on the sentence, paragraph, section, and document level.

SENTENCE-LEVEL UNITY

Singular subjects must be matched with singular verb forms. Plural subjects must be paired with plural verb forms. Although this sounds straightforward, identifying the correct subject of a sentence can be challenging. Consider the following examples:

- Incorrect: "The combined effect of ultraviolet radiation, heat, and heavy metals in the soil were studied."
  Correct: "The combined effect of ultraviolet radiation, heat, and heavy metals in the soil was studied."
  Explanation: The subject in this sentence is "effect," not "ultraviolet radiation, heat, and heavy metals."
- Incorrect: "The recommendation of the committee and the decision of the chairman is final."
  Correct: "The recommendation of the committee and the decision of the chairman are final."
  Explanation: The subjects in this sentence are "recommendation of the committee and decision of the chairman," which require a plural verb.
- Incorrect: "The number of complaints we receive are decreasing."
  Correct: "The number of complaints we receive is decreasing."
  Explanation: The subject in this sentence is "the number," which is singular.

PARAGRAPH-LEVEL UNITY

All sentences of a paragraph should add value to or support the main idea of the paragraph. Sentences that are only peripherally related to the main idea should be organized in a separate paragraph.

Supporting sentences may add the following types of value to the main idea:

- **Evidence:** Data that supports the idea of the paragraph's topic sentence can be presented or discussed in supporting sentences.
- **Examples:** Supporting sentences may be used to give examples of the idea presented in the topic sentence.
- **Clarification:** Definitions of terms used or explanations of concepts mentioned in the topic sentence can be included in supporting sentences.
- **References:** Books, articles, websites, interviews, and other references used in formulating the thesis of the main idea may be mentioned in supporting sentences.
- **Development:** Supporting sentences may build on the main idea in a chronological or logical progression.

In general, the following types of sentences should not be included in a paragraph:

- Sentences that present a view opposing the main idea of the paragraph.
- Sentences that present an idea that will be developed by one or more subsequent paragraphs.
- Sentences more related to the main idea of a previous or subsequent paragraph.

SECTION-LEVEL UNITY

Technical documents are divided into sections. In larger documents, these sections may be formally separated with headings and subheadings. For example, each procedure described in an operations manual may be described in a separate section. In a smaller or informal document, the sections may not be labeled. For example, the introduction, body, and conclusion of the text of a short letter will probably not be labeled with headings.

Each section of a technical document should have a single goal. All paragraphs within the section should be related to that goal. Goals for a section may include:

- introducing the document
- explaining a process, procedure, or concept
- listing materials
- describing a person, place, object, or situation
- requesting money or other resources

DOCUMENT-LEVEL UNITY

In the same way that each paragraph should have a main idea and each section should have a goal, the entire technical document should have a purpose. Examples of purposes of a technical document include:

- complying with local, state, national, or industry regulations
- helping employees perform their job safely or more efficiently
- proposing a solution to a problem
- asking for information or resources

In order to be unified at the document level, each section of the document should support this purpose.

TONE

The **tone** of a document is the way the writer uses sentence structure and vocabulary to convey an attitude toward the subject and the reader. Because the tone of a document will influence the audience's response, technical writers should adopt a tone that will help elicit the desired reader reaction. Tone may be used to:

- encourage readers to form a positive or negative opinion about the subject
- help readers understand a concept
- establish the writer's credibility
- hold the reader's interest
- emphasize or de-emphasize material

One way of setting the tone for a document is through thoughtful use of the active and passive voice. Sentences written in the **active voice** begin with the person or object that performed an action. The recipient of the action follows the verb, as in the following examples:

- The technician collected the samples.
- The construction crew excavated the site.
- The accountant checked the calculations.
- The backhoe removed the tree.

In the **passive voice**, the recipient of the action takes the leading position in the sentence. The person or object performing the action is placed after the verb. The following examples show sentences written in the passive voice.

- The samples were collected by the technician.
- The site was excavated by the construction crew.
- The calculations were checked by the accountant.
- The tree was removed by the backhoe.

Some technical documents, such as instructions and procedures, are usually written in the active voice to help the reader understand who will perform each action. The passive voice may be used in technical documents when the writer needs to give more emphasis to the recipient of an action than to the performer of the action, as in the following examples:

- The samples were destroyed by the process.
- Professor Smith was selected by the committee.
- The patient was transported to University Hospital by helicopter.

The passive voice can be used when the performer of the action is unknown or insignificant.

- The company was awarded the contract.
- The packages were delivered.
- The enzymes were isolated.

The words a writer uses when composing a technical document are important tools in conveying an attitude toward a subject or audience. Vocabulary can be used to create tones such as:

- Disdain toward the subject or audience
- Friendliness toward the audience
- Support for the subject
- Condemnation of the subject
- Neutrality toward the subject
- Respect for the audience

In most situations that require business or technical communication, the writer wants the audience to accept the recommendations of or agree with the document. Readers are less likely to give a positive response when they feel talked down to, insulted, or ignored. For this reason, an effective technical document is likely to include vocabulary that is:

- neither too technical nor too elementary for the likely reader
- professional and courteous
- respectful of the readers' beliefs and current practices

Consider the following excerpt from a procedures manual.

> If you are on the crew, you have to look at your safety card when you start work, when you go to lunch, when you return from lunch, and when you leave for the day. All you have to do is sign and write the time each time you look at the card. Surely everyone can remember to do that much. This does not mean signing the card four times when you get to work. Some people are doing this. You have to know this is wrong and it is not doing anything to keep the workplace safe. There will be periodic card checks, and if your card is not up-to-date or is signed in advance, you will be written up.

The words used in the above passage do not reflect a tone of professionalism, courtesy, and respect. Statements like "surely everyone can remember to do that much," and "you have to know this is wrong" show disdain toward the intended audience. The passage is rewritten below, using vocabulary that is respectful of the reader.

Each crew member must review the appropriate safety card at the following times:

- the beginning of the crew member's shift,
- before the crew member leaves for lunch,
- when the crew member returns from lunch,
- at the end of the crew member's shift.

After each review, the crew member should sign the card and write the time when the card was reviewed. Periodic card checks will be performed to make sure each card is being reviewed appropriately. Crew members whose cards are found to be overdue for a signature or signed in advance may be required to take refresher safety training. Repeat offenses may result in a formal safety violation write-up.

The revised passage better reflects the purpose of the document – to inform the reader about the safety card policy, not to make the reader feel embarrassed or incompetent. From the planning, to the structuring, to the final tone of the document, the audience is the key consideration when writing a technical document.

Sample Test Questions

1) Which of the following is NOT likely to be included in a highly technical document?

   A) Charts, equations, or graphs
   B) Abbreviations that have not been previously defined
   C) Concise answers to questions a reader is likely to ask about the topic
   D) Detailed theoretical background

The correct answer is D:) Detailed theoretical background. Highly technical articles are written for an audience that is already familiar with the topic. Little or no theoretical background is usually needed.

2) An office manager asks for the specifications for a new computer application. Based on the specifications, she decides to purchase the application. After the application is installed, the end users refer to the specifications to see what features are available. Which term best describes the office manager's relationship to the specifications?

   A) Primary reader
   B) Secondary reader
   C) Principle audience
   D) Alternate audience

The correct answer is A:) Primary reader. The primary audience of a piece of technical writing requests the material and uses it to make decisions.

3) Choose the best revision for the sentence below. If the sentence does not need to be revised, choose answer A). "We set sail, pushed off the shore, and looked for fish until sunset."

   A) "We set sail, pushed off the shore, and looked for fish until sunset."
   B) "We set sail and pushed off the shore, then looked for fish until sunset."
   C) "Until sunset, we set sail, pushed off the shore, and looked for fish."
   D) "We set sail, we pushed off the shore, and we looked for fish until sunset."

The correct answer is B:) "We set sail and pushed off the shore, then looked for fish until sunset." The original sentence is ambiguous as to whether the writer set sail and pushed off the shore once or multiple times until sunset. The correct answer clears the ambiguity.

4) What is the main purpose of a technical proposal?

    A) Persuasion
    B) Instruction
    C) Communication
    D) Research

The correct answer is A:) Persuasion. Technical proposals are used to persuade readers to take a specified course of action.

5) A list of average daily temperatures for a city is an example of which type of source?

    A) Primary
    B) Secondary
    C) Major
    D) Minor

The correct answer is A:) Primary. Records of transactions, measurements, and experiments are examples of primary sources.

6) What two stages best describe an analysis?

    A) Define and describe
    B) Compare and contrast
    C) Divide and discuss
    D) Partition and classify

The correct answer is D:) Partition and classify. To analyze a subject is to divide it into segments and then classify those segments based on their similarities.

7) What is the name for a graphic element that is a list of non-numeric information arranged in rows and columns?

    A) Figure
    B) Table
    C) Chart
    D) Graph

The correct answer is B:) Table. A table may contain numeric information, non-numeric information, or both.

8) A coordinate system is required for which type of graphic?

    A) Figure
    B) Table
    C) Chart
    D) Graph

The correct answer is D:) Graph. A graph shows quantifiable information charted on a coordinate system.

9) What is the most likely explanation for an asterisk after a word in a technical document?

    A) The reader should refer to the footnotes
    B) The word is defined in the glossary
    C) There are qualifications connected to the word
    D) The word is a direct quote from another source

The correct answer is B:) The word is defined in the glossary. Terms defined in an attached glossary can be designated by an asterisk.

10) What term would refer to the empty space on a document printed on blue paper?

    A) White space
    B) Blue space
    C) Negative space
    D) Blank space

The correct answer is A:) White space. White space refers to any areas without text or graphics.

11) Which is true about the x-height of a typeface?

    A) It is the height of a capital X
    B) It is the height of the main body of a lowercase letter
    C) It is the height of a lowercase letter
    D) None of the above

The correct answer is B:) It is the height of the main body of a lowercase letter. The x-height of a typeface is the height of a lowercase letter x in that type. That is equal to the height of the main body of any lowercase letter in that type.

12) Which of the following is most likely to be found in an appendix?

    A) List of materials used to research the document
    B) Definitions of technical terms used in the document
    C) Transcripts of interviews referenced in the document
    D) The body of the document

The correct answer is C): Transcripts of interviews referenced in the document. Appendices supply details about material discussed in the document.

13) The notation "WW/tt" would most likely be found at the bottom left hand corner on what type of document?

    A) Letter
    B) Report
    C) Analysis
    D) Proposal

The correct answer is A:) Letter. If the letter is not physically typed by the person signing the document, the typist initials should be placed two lines below the signature and aligned at the left margin.

14) Which is true about the format of a resume?

    A) The work experience section should come before the education section
    B) The education section should come before the work experience section
    C) The stronger section should come first
    D) The weaker section should come first

The correct answer is C:) The stronger section should come first. Applicants should arrange their resumes to highlight the stronger of their work experience or educational background.

15) Which of the following is true about a document that is written in the first person and describes how the writer completed a titration experiment?

    A) The document is a process analysis
    B) The document is a set of instructions
    C) The document is a process narrative
    D) The document is a procedure

The correct answer is C:) The document is a process narrative. A process narrative is a writer-oriented process description.

16) Which of the following are reader-oriented?

  A) Process analyses
  B) Process narratives
  C) Process instructions
  D) They are all reader-oriented

The correct answer is C:) Process instructions. Process analyses are subject-oriented and process narratives are writer-oriented. Process instructions are directions for completing a process from the reader's point of view.

17) Which sentence is written in the imperative mood?

  A) "You open the stove when the temperature is reached."
  B) "You need to open the stove when the temperature is reached."
  C) "Open the stove when the temperature is reached."
  D) Both A and B

The correct answer is C:) "Open the stove when the temperature is reached." If the subject of the sentences is an understood you, the mood is imperative.

18) Which is the most appropriate example of documentation from a research paper?

  A) "According to Stoughton, parallelism is achieved by balancing words or phrases with other words and phrases that are of the same type (Stoughton, 109)."
  B) "According to Stoughton, parallelism is achieved by balancing words or phrases with other words and phrases that are of the same type (109)."
  C) "According to Stoughton, parallelism is achieved by balancing words or phrases with other words and phrases that are of the same type. (Stoughton, 109)"
  D) "According to Stoughton, parallelism is achieved by balancing words or phrases with other words and phrases that are of the same type. (109)"

The correct answer is B:) "According to Stoughton, parallelism is achieved by balancing words or phrases with other words and phrases that are of the same type (109)." When the author is already identified in the text, the information does not have to be repeated in the parenthetical documentation.

19) Which is true about a highly technical presentation strategy?

    A) A highly technical presentation strategy should be used when the reader's technical background is likely to be the same as the writer's.
    B) A highly technical presentation strategy is used whenever the reader needs technical details about the subject.
    C) A highly technical presentation strategy is reserved for technical fields such as science, mathematics, and engineering.
    D) A highly technical presentation strategy includes detailed explanations of raw data.

The correct answer is A:) A highly technical presentation strategy should be used when the reader's technical background is likely to be the same as the writer's. The presentation strategy used depends on the relationship between the writer's and audience's experience and expertise.

20) When planning a technical document, a writer is likely to organize the project requirements on what type of form?

    A) A document preparation sheet
    B) A technical brief
    C) A project specification outline
    D) A project summary

The correct answer is B:) A technical brief. A technical brief is a worksheet used by technical writers to organize project specification and notes about the intended audience.

21) Which term best describes a guided online conversation between a group of people similar to the intended audience of a document for the purpose of researching reader needs?

    A) An online survey
    B) An online interview
    C) A focus group
    D) A structured interview

The correct answer is C:) A focus group. A focus group may be held online or in person. Group interaction may reveal issues the researcher had not considered.

22) What is the main purpose of a report?

    A) To communicate with the reader
    B) To list general information about a subject
    C) To find connections between sets of data
    D) All of the above

The correct answer is A:) To communicate with the reader. A report is used to communicate a recommendation, result, opinion, or conclusion to an internal or external audience.

23) Which is most likely to be true about a progress report?

    A) It is written by the organization working on the project
    B) It is written by the organization funding, commissioning, or overseeing the project
    C) It is prepared to hold the contractor accountable to the schedule
    D) It is an internal document

The correct answer is A:) It is written by the organization working on the project. A progress report usually generates from the organization, department, or person working on the project. When the report comes from the client, it is called an inspection report.

24) Which term refers to a document that communicates an opinion about a proposed solution to a problem?

    A) Solution report
    B) Proposal
    C) Recommendation report
    D) Feasibility report

The correct answer is D:) Feasibility report. A feasibility report answers questions about the practicality of a proposed solution.

25) Requirements examined in a formal feasibility report may be defined according to what type of strategy?

    A) Statistical
    B) Rating
    C) Evaluation
    D) Logarithmic

The correct answer is B:) Rating. A feasibility report may define criteria using numerical, yes/no, or rating strategies.

26) A report compares two possible courses of action, X and Y. First the characteristics of X are discussed, then the characteristics of Y. What term best describes this approach?

A) Part-to-part comparison
B) Delineated comparison
C) Whole-to-whole comparison
D) Whole-entity analysis

The correct answer is C:) Whole-to-whole comparison. In a whole-to-whole comparison, the qualities of an entire entity are examined before moving to the next entity.

27) A conclusion that balances several simple conclusions about individual requirements is known as what kind of conclusion?

A) Primary
B) Secondary
C) Tertiary
D) Final

The correct answer is B:) Secondary. A secondary conclusion combines several primary conclusions. For example, "Although Option X can be completed the quickest, Option Y is less expensive."

28) Which element of a laboratory report is most likely to appear first in the final document?

A) Abstract
B) Executive summary
C) Introduction
D) Methodology

The correct answer is A:) Abstract. A laboratory report usually opens with a short abstract that summarizes the major points of the document.

29) Which statement is true about a memorandum?

A) A memorandum is an example of formal correspondence
B) A memorandum is an example of informal correspondence
C) A memorandum should include background information and supplemental material
D) A memorandum is usually an external document

The correct answer is B:) A memorandum is an example of informal correspondence. A memo is usually reserved for informal internal correspondence.

30) Which of the following is not likely to be communicated using a memo?

   A) Research results
   B) Schedules
   C) Proposals
   D) Receipts

The correct answer is D:) Receipts. Receipts are likely to be external documents. Memos are used for internal communication.

31) If a letter is not physically typed by the person signing the document, which of the following should be added?

   A) Typist's verification
   B) Typist's name
   C) Typist's initials
   D) Typist's notation

The correct answer is C:) Typist's initials. The writer's initials are written in capital letters, followed by a slash and the typist's initials in lowercase letters.

32) The label "cc:" is used in which element of a formal letter?

   A) Distribution notation
   B) Recipient notation
   C) Carbon/blind copy verification
   D) Distribution verification

The correct answer is A:) Distribution notation. The distribution notation is used to disclose to the recipient of the letter who else received a copy of the letter.

33) In what letter format is the first line of each paragraph indented?

   A) Semiblock
   B) Modified block
   C) Block
   D) None of the above

The correct answer is B:) Modified block. In modified block format, the letter text is single spaced with a double spacing between paragraphs. The first line of each paragraph is indented.

34) A formal request for information about a procedure can be sent using what type of letter?

    A) Inquiry
    B) Instruction
    C) Request
    D) Appeal

The correct answer is A:) Inquiry. A letter of inquiry is used to ask for information about a product, service, or procedure.

35) What is a main objective of a job application letter?

    A) To present an image
    B) To list the writer's accomplishments
    C) To list the writer's experiences
    D) All of the above

The correct answer is A:) To present an image. Lists of accomplishments and experiences should be included in the résumé, not the job application letter.

36) Which of the following could be an audience for a manual?

    A) Consumers
    B) Technicians
    C) Professionals
    D) All of the above

The correct answer is D:) All of the above. Manuals may be written for any group of readers that need to use, understand, or maintain an object.

37) Which of the following is a descriptive sequence that could be used in a manual?

    A) Progressive sequence
    B) Spatial sequence
    C) Absolute sequence
    D) Instructional sequence

The correct answer is B:) Spatial sequence. Descriptive sequences may be spatial, chronological, functional, or combination.

38) If a tape recorder is described in the order the parts were assembled, what type of descriptive sequence is used?

    A) Manufacturing sequence
    B) Objective sequence
    C) Assembly sequence
    D) Chronological sequence

The correct answer is D:) Chronological sequence. A chronological sequence orders the parts based on the assembly process.

39) Which of the following is true about instructions?

    A) Instructions are writer-oriented
    B) Instructions are object-oriented
    C) Instructions are reader-oriented
    D) Instructions are process-oriented

The correct answer is C:) Instructions are reader-oriented. Instructions are reader-oriented directions for completing a task.

40) Which of the following is true about instructions?

    A) Instructions are written in the active voice
    B) Instructions are written in the passive voice
    C) Instructions are written in the indicative mood
    D) Instructions are written in the declarative mood

The correct answer is A:) Instructions are written in the active voice. Instructions are easier to understand if they are written in the active voice and imperative mood.

41) Which of the following sentences is written in the imperative mood?

    A) "You need to mix the eggs and water."
    B) "You should mix the eggs and water."
    C) "Mix the eggs and water."
    D) "It is imperative that you mix the eggs and water."

The correct answer is C:) "Mix the eggs and water." The imperative mood uses the understood you.

42) Which of the following sentences uses a parallel structure?

   A) "Applicants should have good technical skills, a degree in science, be able to type, and a good work ethic."
   B) "Applicants should have good technical skills, a degree in science, be able to type, and have a good work ethic."
   C) "Applicants should have good technical skills and a degree in science, be able to type, and possess a good work ethic."
   D) "Applicants should have good technical skills, possess a degree in science, typing skills, and a good work ethic."

The correct answer is C:) "Applicants should have good technical skills and a degree in science, be able to type, and possess a good work ethic." Parallel structure means each element in a group is equivalent grammatically. In the correct answer, each element in the list begins with a verb.

43) Which term refers to rules that govern processes in an organization?

   A) Policies
   B) Procedures
   C) Principles
   D) Both A and B

The correct answer is A:) Policies. Policies are rules that govern processes. Procedures are ways policies are implemented.

44) Which is true about a procedure?

   A) A procedure should use names, addresses and telephone numbers
   B) A procedure is only written for administrators
   C) A procedure should offer some benefit to the user
   D) A procedure should be as restrictive as possible to provide adequate structure

The correct answer is C:) A procedure should offer some benefit to the user. Procedures should be written so that the user is benefited by following the procedure. Benefits may include being able to complete a task more easily, more securely, or in safer conditions.

45) Which of the following should NOT be included in the header of a written procedure?

A) The title of the procedure
B) The date the procedure for take effect
C) The office that approved the procedure
D) The objectives of the procedure

The correct answer is D:) The objectives of the procedure. The objectives are listed in the overview section.

46) Procedure bodies are written in what format?

A) Paragraphs
B) Checklists
C) Worksheets
D) Any of the above

The correct answer is D:) Any of the above. A procedure body is written in a format that meets the organization requirements, is approachable to the intended audience, and is appropriate to the related policy.

47) Which of the following is a type of process description?

A) Process narrative
B) Process analysis
C) Process report
D) Both A and B

The correct answer is D:) Both A and B. A process description may be written as a narrative or an analysis.

48) Which term is used for a process description that is written in the first person?

A) Process narrative
B) Process analysis
C) Process report
D) Process account

The correct answer is A:) Process narrative. A process narrative is a firsthand account that emphasizes the writer's role.

49) What term best describes a technical document that is written to convince the reader to take a certain action?

A) Proposition
B) Proposal
C) Recommendation
D) Persuasion

The correct answer is B:) Proposal. A proposal is written to persuade the reader to take a specific action, such as using a contractor or purchasing equipment.

50) The problem is defined in which section of a proposal?

A) Statement of problem
B) Statement of purpose
C) Background
D) Objectives

The correct answer is A:) Statement of problem. A description of the problem that needs to be solved is included in the statement of problem section.

51) A business report is most likely to include what element?

A) Narrative
B) Abstract
C) Executive summary
D) Limitations

The correct answer is C:) Executive summary. Business documents are likely to include executive summaries. Abstracts are used in scientific documents.

52) Section headings should be which of the following

A) Parallel
B) Cohesive
C) Concrete
D) Both A and B

The correct answer is D:) Both A and B. Section headings should following a parallel and cohesive organization scheme.

53) Which of the following should NOT be included in a definition section?

    A) Terms with abstract definitions
    B) Terms often used in the industry
    C) Job titles specific to the organization
    D) Terms with ambiguous meanings

The correct answer is B) Terms often used in the industry. The definition section should not include terms the audience is likely to be familiar with.

54) Which statement best describes the term "begging the question"?

    A) A conclusion is based on a piece of evidence that is a restatement of the conclusion
    B) Two things are compared that are alike in some ways, but not in ways that are important to the argument
    C) A tangential issue is addressed to distract the reader from the main question
    D) A conclusion is drawn that is more extreme than the evidence supports

The correct answer is A:) A conclusion is based on a piece of evidence that is a restatement of the conclusion. To beg the question means to base the conclusion on evidence that restates the question or to ignore critical flaws in a piece of evidence.

55) Which statement refers to an argument that relies on public opinion to support a position?

    A) *Ad populum*
    B) *Ad hominem*
    C) *Tu quoque*
    D) *Post hoc*

The correct answer is A:) *Ad populum*. An *ad populum* argument assumes that the majority opinion is the best one.

56) What term refers to a conclusion that is reached through a fault in deductive reasoning?

    A) Untruthful
    B) Invalid
    C) False
    D) Artificial

The correct answer is B:) Invalid. Validity refers to the strength of the logic behind a conclusion.

57) Which of the following are two categories of graphic elements?

   A) Graphs and illustrations
   B) Tables and figures
   C) Illustrations and tables
   D) Charts and pictures

The correct answer is B:) Tables and figures. Graphics are divided into tables and figures.

58) Which term refers to a bar graph divided into constituent parts?

   A) Divided bar graph
   B) Sectional bar graph
   C) Stacked bar graph
   D) Fragmented bar graph

The correct answer is C:) Stacked bar graph. A stacked or segmented bar graph divided categories into components.

59) Which statement best describes a line graph?

   A) The dependent axis must be quantifiable
   B) The independent axis must be quantifiable
   C) The dependent axis must be numerical
   D) Both axes must be quantifiable

The correct answer is D:) Both axes must be quantifiable. In a line graph, both the horizontal and vertical axes must be based on quantifiable measurements.

60) Which statement best describes a chart?

   A) The independent axis of a chart must be quantifiable
   B) Charts illustrate relative size or positions
   C) Charts show the change in quantities over time
   D) Charts use a coordinate system to show information

The correct answer is B:) Charts illustrate relative size or positions. A chart shows the relationship between two or more data types. They are based on relative, not actual, quantities.

61) Which of the following is true about pie charts?

   A) Each section of a pie chart represents a category of information
   B) Pie charts are graphed on a coordinate axis
   C) Pie charts are graphed on a polar axis
   D) Both A and C

The correct answer is A:) Each section of a pie chart represents a category of information. Pie charts are used to show the composition percentage of each category. The relative size of each section represents the category's percentage of the whole.

62) Which type of chart shows the decisions involved in completing a process?

   A) Organizational charts
   B) Flowcharts
   C) Decision charts
   D) Process charts

The correct answer is B:) Flowcharts. Flowcharts are used to walk readers through the steps involved in a task.

63) Which term refers to an illustration of how parts of an object fit together?

   A) Component diagram
   B) Constituent diagram
   C) Element diagram
   D) Exploded diagram

The correct answer is D:) Exploded diagram. An exploded diagram shows the component parts slightly separated from each other so the reader can better understand how the elements fit together.

64) Which term refers to a simplified definition of the term that is useful within the scope of the document?

   A) Working definition
   B) Bounded definition
   C) Standard definition
   D) Unbounded definition

The correct answer is A:) Working definition. When a working definition is used in a technical document, it should be stated the first time the term is used.

65) Which type of terms should NOT be included in a glossary?

    A) Terms the primary audience is unlikely to understand
    B) Terms the secondary audience is unlikely to understand
    C) Terms used in unusual ways in the document
    D) Specialized terms that the audience is likely to understand

The correct answer is D:) Specialized terms that the audience is likely to understand. A glossary is used to help readers understand specialized term that they are unlikely to be familiar with.

66) What is NOT a possible use of footnotes?

    A) To provide bibliographic information
    B) To explain missing data in a table
    C) To explain complicated methodology or background information
    D) To provide minor or tangential details

The correct answer is C:) To explain complicated methodology or background information. Long discussions about background information should be placed in an appendix.

67) Which is NOT true of appendices?

    A) They may contain tables that are too large to be printed on one page
    B) They may contain background information that is probably unfamiliar to the secondary audience
    C) They may contain background information that is probably familiar to the primary audience
    D) They are labeled numerically

The correct answer is D:) They are labeled numerically. Appendices are labeled with consecutive capital letters.

68) Which of the following is NOT a characteristic used to categorize letter types?

    A) X-height
    B) Y-width
    C) Cap height
    D) Bowl

The correct answer is B:) Y-width. X-height describes the height of a lowercase x. Cap height refers to the height of uppercase letters. Bowl describes the empty space inside rounded uppercase letters.

69) Which term refers to the graphics on a page?

A) White space
B) Gray space
C) Black space
D) Brown space

The correct answer is C:) Black space. White space refers to areas without text or graphics. Gray space describes areas with text.

70) Which is NOT true about reading text on a computer screen?

A) Reading a long passage on a computer screen is facilitated by using multiple columns
B) Reading a long passage on a computer screen is more fatiguing than reading the same passage on a sheet of paper
C) How a passage appears on a computer screen depends on the hardware and software being used
D) Both A and C

The correct answer is A:) Reading a long passage on a computer screen is facilitated by using multiple columns. Using more than one column on an electronic document may force the reader to scroll more to access the entire passage. Increased scrolling can be fatiguing and frustrating for the reader.

71) A scientist wants to distribute an electronic document in a format that allows each reader to edit and redistribute the document. Which format would be the most appropriate choice?

A) Text file
B) Html file
C) Portable document format
D) Flash file

The correct answer is A:) Text file. Text files can be opened and edited by any user with a word processing application.

72) Writers of technical material should consider which of the following types of audiences?

    A) Primary audience only
    B) Primary and secondary audiences
    C) Audience only
    D) Principle and alternate audiences

The correct answer is B:) Primary and secondary audiences. Technical writers must consider all readers who are likely to use the material.

73) Which term is used to refer to the degree to which the structure of a document helps the document be used by readers?

    A) Completeness
    B) Accessibility
    C) Utility
    D) Structure

The correct answer is B:) Accessibility. Accessibility refers to the way vocabulary, sentence structure, and page layout helps readers use a document.

74) Choose the best revision for the sentence below.

"A technician should not attempt the procedure until he has completed the required training."

    A) No change.
    B) "Until he has completed the required training, a technician should avoid attempting the procedure."
    C) "The procedure should not be attempted until the technician has completed the required procedure."
    D) "Technicians should not attempt the procedure until they have completed the required training."

The correct answer is D:) "Technicians should not attempt the procedure until they have completed the required training." Sexist language should be avoided in technical documents. Although the singular pronoun is avoided in answer C, the passive voice removes the impact of the statement.

75) Which of the following is a complex sentence?

    A) "Without the correct reagent, we will not be able to finish the experiment."
    B) "Without the correct reagent, we will not be able to finish the experiment and will have to cut the project short."
    C) "We will not be able to finish the experiment and will have to cut the project short."
    D) "We will not be able to finish the experiment."

The correct answer is A:) "Without the correct reagent, we will not be able to finish the experiment." A complex sentence has one independent clause and one or more subordinate clauses. In the correct answer, the independent clause is "we will not be able to finish the experiment." The subordinate clause is "without the correct reagent."

76) Which of the following is most likely to make a document more accessible to readers?

    A) Using a sans serif typeface
    B) Aligning the right margin
    C) Aligning the left margin
    D) Decreasing the margins

The correct answer is C:) Aligning the left margin. Aligning the left margin and leaving the right margin ragged helps audiences read text more comfortably. Using a serif typeface and wider margins can also make a document easier to read.

77) Which type of process explanation emphasizes the reader's role in the task?

    A) Instructions
    B) Narratives
    C) Analyses
    D) Procedures

The correct answer is A:) Instructions. Process explanations may be instructions, narratives, or analyses. Instructions emphasize the reader's role. Narratives emphasize the writer's role. Analyses emphasize the process.

78) Which term is used to describe a division that divides a single element into parts?

    A) Organization
    B) Cataloging
    C) Classification
    D) Partition

The correct answer is D:) Partition. A partition is used to divide a single element into parts. Classification is the process of sorting similar elements into categories.

79) What term is used to describe evidence based on opinion?

    A) Soft
    B) Fragile
    C) Weak
    D) Delicate

The correct answer is A:) Soft. Soft evidence is supported by opinion. Hard evidence is support by verifiable facts.

80) What term is used to describe a letter sent in response to a request or advertisement?

    A) Formal
    B) Solicited
    C) Responsive
    D) Reactive

The correct answer is B:) Solicited. Solicited letters are expected by the recipients, either because they asked for information from the sender personally or through a general correspondence.

81) Choose the best revision for the sentence below.

"All things considered, the results suggest that the best option is to keep the POS system that we currently have."

A) No change.
B) "The results suggest that the best option is to keep the POS system we currently have."
C) "The results suggest that the best option is to keep the current POS system."
D) "All things considered, the results suggest that the best option is to keep the current POS system."

The correct answer is C:) "The results suggest that the best option is to keep the current POS system." Concise language is more engaging to the reader. Phrases such as "all things considered" seldom add value to a sentence.

82) Which of the following sentences is structured to emphasize the word "clients"?

A) "Clients are considered first in any scheduling decisions."
B) "We confer with the clients before making any scheduling decisions."
C) "Before making any scheduling decisions, we confer with the clients."
D) A and C give equal emphasis to the word "client."

The correct answer is D:) A and C give equal emphasis to the word "client." Words are given more emphasis when they are moved to the beginning or end of a sentence.

83) Choose the best revision for the sentence below.

"Because it was built under budget, the benefits of the parking facility's new payment system is likely to be worth the expense."

A) No change.
B) "Because it was built under budget, the benefits of the parking facility's new payment system are likely to be worth the expense."
C) "Because the parking facility was built under budget, the benefits of its new payment system are likely to be worth the expense."
D) "Because the parking facility was built under budget, the benefits of the parking facility's new payment system are likely to be worth the expense."

The correct answer is C:) "Because the parking facility was built under budget, the benefits of its new payment system are likely to be worth the expense." In the original sentence, the plural subject "benefits" is paired with the singular verb "is. There is also ambiguity about what the word "it" refers to. The correct answer revises the sentence for unity and clears the ambiguity without unneeded words.

84) Which of the following is true about the passive voice?

A) The passive voice should never be used in a technical document
B) The passive voice is used to help readers understand who will be performing each task
C) The passive voice is used to emphasize how a task was completed
D) The passive voice is used to emphasize the recipient of an action

The correct answer is D:) The passive voice is used to emphasize the recipient of an action. The passive voice can be used when the performer of an action is not important.

85) Choose the best revision for the sentence below.

"Besides a small increase in yearly tuition, the budget cut has not seemed to affect the school's operations."

A) No change.
B) "Besides a small increase in yearly tuition, the budget cut has not seemed to effect the school's operations."
C) "Beside a small increase in yearly tuition, the budget cut has not seemed to affect the school's operations."
D) "Beside a small increase in yearly tuition, the budget cut has not seemed to effect the school's operations."

The correct answer is A:) No change. "Beside" means "next to." "Besides" means "other than" or "in addition to." "Effect" is a noun. "Affect" is a verb.

86) Which of the following elements is likely to be included in the body of a formal proposal?

A) Methods
B) Personnel
C) Available facilities
D) All of the above

The correct answer is D:) All of the above. The body of a formal proposal is likely to include subsections that explain the details of the proposed solution, including how the solution will be achieved, who will work on the proposed process, and what facilities are available to devote to the solution.

87) What is the result of inconsistent spacing on the x-axis of a line graph?

A) The data points will not be connected
B) The graph will be distorted
C) The graph will not be able to accommodate all data points
D) All of the above

The correct answer is B:) The graph will be distorted. A line graph with uneven spacing in the x-axis will not be an accurate representation of the data.

88) Which of the following is a compound sentence?

   A) "The sample was heated and put in the centrifuge."
   B) "After the reagents were added, the sample was heated and put in the centrifuge."
   C) "After the reagents were added, the sample was heated."
   D) "The sample was heated."

The correct answer is A:) "The sample was heated and put in the centrifuge." A compound sentence contains two or more independent clauses. In this sentence, the independent clauses are "the sample was heated," and "the sample was put in the centrifuge."

89) A computer application is described in the following sequence: loading the application, using the application, saving work, exiting the application. Which description sequence was used?

   A) Spatial
   B) Chronological
   C) Functional
   D) Combination

The correct answer is C:) Functional. A functional sequence describes an item's features in the order they are used.

90) A writer identifies a group of potential readers. She meets with each member of the group individually. During the meeting, she asks a few short answer questions and records the responses. What research method did the writer use?

   A) Verbal survey
   B) Structured interview
   C) Focus group
   D) Written questionnaire

The correct answer is A:) Verbal survey. A structured interview relies on open-ended questions, not short-answer questions. In a focus group, members of the group can interact with each other while answering questions. Because the questions were asked verbally, the research method was not a written questionnaire.

91) What is an advantage of using a written questionnaire when researching the intended audience for a technical document?

    A) Participants may answer more honestly
    B) Participants will try to appear their best
    C) Answers can be interpreted more leniently
    D) The open-ended questions encourage participant discussion

The correct answer is A:) Participants may answer more honestly. Because participants are not face-to-face with a researcher, they may be less concerned with how their responses will be judged.

92) What is the format error in the following footnote?

[3] David A. Lauer and Stephen Pentak, <u>Design Basics</u> (Harbrace: Orlando, 2000) 17.

    A) There is no error
    B) "2000" is in the wrong position
    C) "17" is in the wrong position
    D) "Orlando" is in the wrong position

The correct answer is D:) "Orlando" is in the wrong position. The city of publication is listed before the brief name of the publisher. The correct format of the footnote is:

[3] David A. Lauer and Stephen Pentak, <u>Design Basics</u> (Orlando: Harbrace, 2000) 17.

93) What term refers to leaving an even amount of space between each letter in a publication?

    A) Kerning
    B) Leading
    C) Tracking
    D) Lining

The correct answer is C:) Tracking. Both kerning and tracking refer to the space between the letters in a line of print. However, kerning adjusts the amount of spaced based on the letters involved. Tracking maintains an even space between all letters.

94) A report about the performance of a client's stock portfolio contains a two-page table listing each stock's quarterly performance. Where should the table be placed?

A) As close as possible to its reference in the text of the report
B) In an appendix
C) In the centerfold of the published report
D) Immediately after the body of the report

The correct answer is B:) In an appendix. Tables and figures that can not be contained on one page should be placed in appendices.

95) An engineer is writing a feasibility report about a proposal to install a new walkway at a city park. A description of the pedestrian traffic at the park should be included in which section?

A) Introduction
B) Technical background
C) Situation background
D) Requirements

The correct answer is C:) Situation background. Details about the problem that will be solved by the proposed solution should be included in the situation background.

96) What is the general purpose of a process description?

A) To compartmentalize the tasks involved in a process
B) To explain the reader's role in a process
C) To explain the component parts of a process
D) To describe the causes and effects of a process

The correct answer is D:) To describe the causes and effects of a process. A process description describes what leads up to each task in a process, and how that task affects the whole.

97) The steps in a process description should be listed in what order?

    A) Spatial
    B) Chronological
    C) Functional
    D) It depends on the process being described

The correct answer is B:) Chronological. Steps in a process description should be presented in the order they occur.

98) Which of the following is the most appropriate title for a laboratory report?

    A) "Honeybees and Lawn Mowing"
    B) "The Correlation Between Lawn Care Practices and Honeybee Populations in Midwestern Rural Communities"
    C) "Where Have All the Honeybees Gone?"
    D) "High Mowing Frequency, Increased Pesticide Use, Low Grass Length, and Decreased Naturalization Are Reducing Populations of *Apis cerana* in the Rural Midwest"

The correct answer is B:) "The Correlation Between Lawn Care Practices and Honeybee Populations in Midwestern Rural Communities." The title of a technical report should state the entities being studied and the relationship between the entities. Summaries of the writer's conclusions should not be included in the title.

99) What is the function of section headings?

    A) To break up gray space
    B) To help readers skim documents
    C) To show relationships between concepts
    D) All of the above

The correct answer is D:) All of the above. Section headings break up blocks of text, help readers pinpoint the information they are looking for, and provide a framework for organizing material.

100) What term refers to bands of white space at the top of a publication?

    A) Sinks
    B) Bleeds
    C) Borders
    D) Rules

The correct answer is A:) Sinks. Sinks, or "drops," are borders of white space at the top of publications. Bleeds are graphics that extend to the edge of the paper. Borders are rectangles of black space. Rules are lines used to separate elements on a page.

101) The term RFP refers to what?

    A) Request for proposal
    B) Recently forbidden prospectus
    C) Request for proof
    D) Request for personel

The correct answer is A:) Request for proposal. An RFP is generally used to request pricing or information from a large variety of suppliers or sources.

102) Which of the following would be best demonstrated on a bar graph?

    A) To show the relationship between cost of a product and sales of that product
    B) To display the results of a poll asking people what their favorite season is
    C) To show the sequence for developing computer chips
    D) To show the proportion of students who are achieving an "A" grade in relation to the whole class

The correct answer is B:) To display the results of a poll asking people what their favorite season is. Bar graphs are particularly helpful when one of the variables is qualitative rather than quantitative, such as seasons.

103) Which of the following MOST closely means vague or unclear?

    A) Concise
    B) Ambiguous
    C) Jargon
    D) Distinct

The correct answer is B:) Ambiguous. If something is ambiguous then the meaning is unclear, and it could be interpreted in multiple ways. This makes ambiguous the correct answer.

104) Which of the following MOST closely describes the word concise?

A) Succinct, brief, to the point
B) Vague, unclear
C) Lengthy, drawn out, detailed
D) Confusing, strange, different

The correct answer is A:) Succinct, brief, to the point. If something is concise then it is stated in a very clear and straightforward way.

105) A sentence in which the subject performs the action is written in

A) Lengthy voice
B) Passive voice
C) Concise voice
D) Active voice

The correct answer is D:) Active voice. For example, the statement "Jonathan ran to the store" is in the active voice because the subject, Jonathan, is performing the action.

106) A sentence in which the subject receives the action is written in

A) Active voice
B) Receptive voice
C) Passive voice
D) Descriptive voice

The correct answer is C:) Passive voice. For example, the statement "The letter was mailed to Jonathan" is written in the passive voice because Jonathan is not identified as performing the action, but as receiving it.

107) Which of the following would be best demonstrated on a flow chart?

A) To show the relationship between cost of a product and sales of that product
B) To display the results of a poll asking people what their favorite season is
C) To show the sequence for developing computer chips
D) To show the proportion of students who are achieving an "A" grade in relation to the whole class

The correct answer is D:) To show the proportion of students who are achieving an "A" grade in relation to the whole class. Pie graphs are used to show proportional relationships between variables. This means that the best use of a pie graph would be for option D.

108) Language specific to a certain field is known as

    A) Jargon
    B) Appendix
    C) Ambiguous
    D) Definitive

The correct answer is A:) Jargon. Jargon is typically used in technical fields such as medicine or technology in which there are many terms that are unique to specific tasks.

109) Which of the following BEST describes what a summary is?

    A) Additional information at the end of a publication
    B) A brief description of certain information that highlights the main points
    C) A sentence in which the subject is performing an action
    D) A drawn-out proof of stated facts

The correct answer is B:) A brief description of information that highlights the main points.

110) Writing which considers the causes and effects of a situation is known as

    A) Causal analysis
    B) Functional analysis
    C) Concise analysis
    D) Discrete analysis

The correct answer is A:) Causal analysis. Analysis which breaks a problem into smaller components to be individually analyzed is known as functional analysis. Analysis which considers primarily the causes of a problem is known as causal analysis.

111) Which of the following would be best demonstrated on a scatter plot?

    A) To show the relationship between cost of a product and sales of that product
    B) To display the results of a poll asking people what their favorite season is
    C) To show the sequence for developing computer chips
    D) To show the proportion of students who are achieving an "A" grade in relation to the whole class

The correct answer is A:) To show the relationship between cost of a product and sales of that product. Scatter plots are very effective in showing the correlation between two numerical quantities. The best example of this is option A.

112) Where can you find the appendix to a report?

    A) Before the introduction
    B) At the bottom of each page
    C) At the end of the document
    D) Anywhere is acceptable as long as it is clearly identified

The correct answer is C:) At the end of the document. An appendix is used to include more detailed information that can't be described in the actual paper. Therefore, it is placed at the end of the document so that the reader can reference it if they wish to.

113) Which of the following would you NOT include in a cover letter?

    A) A description of why you want to
    B) Details about your education
    C) Your contact information
    D) A salutation

The correct answer is B:) Details about your education. The purpose of the cover letter is to provide a summary of why you are qualified for and desire a certain job. Details such as education, experience, and so forth would be found in a resume.

114) Which of the following can function as a grammatically correct sentence?

    A) Dependent clause
    B) Sentence fragment
    C) Independent clause
    D) Run-on

The correct answer is C:) Independent clause. A complete sentence must have a subject, a predicate, and express a complete thought. Of the options given, only an independent clause satisfies those three requirements.

115) Which of the following demonstrates the proper punctuation for a salutation?

    A) Dear Mr. Smith-
    B) Dear Mr. Smith;
    C) Dear Mr. Smith,
    D) Dear Mr. Smith:

The correct answer is D:) Dear Mr. Smith:. The semicolon is the proper way to punctuate a salutation.

116) Where would the reference list be found in a paper?

    A) In the introduction
    B) In the abstract
    C) At the end
    D) None of the above

The correct answer is C:) At the end. References should be noted in the body of the paper, and the reference list with more information should be at the end.

117) Which of the following would be best demonstrated on a flow chart?

    A) To show the relationship between cost of a product and sales of that product
    B) To display the results of a poll asking people what their favorite season is
    C) To show the sequence for developing computer chips
    D) To show the proportion of students who are achieving an "A" grade in relation to the whole class

The correct answer is C:) To show the sequence for developing computer chips. A flow chart is best used to show a sequence of events or a process. This makes option C the most correct answer.

Test Taking Strategies

Here are some test-taking strategies that are specific to this test and to other DSST tests in general:

- Keep your eyes on the time. Pay attention to how much time you have left.

- Read the entire question and read all the answers. Many questions are not as hard to answer as they may seem. Sometimes, a difficult sounding question really only is asking you how to read an accompanying chart. Chart and graph questions are on most DANTES/DSST tests and should be an easy free point.

- If you don't know the answer immediately, the new computer-based testing lets you mark questions and come back to them later if you have time.

- Read the wording carefully. Some words can give you hints to the right answer. There are no exceptions to an answer when there are words in the question such as always, all or none. If one of the answer choices includes most or some of the right answers, but not all, then that is not the answer. Here is an example:

The primary colors include all of the following:

A) Red, Yellow, Blue, Green

B) Red, Green, Yellow

C) Red, Orange, Yellow

D) Red, Yellow, Blue

Although item A includes all the right answers, it also includes an incorrect answer, making it incorrect. If you didn't read it carefully, were in a hurry, or didn't know the material well, you might fall for this.

- Make a guess on a question that you do not know the answer to. There is no penalty for an incorrect answer. Eliminate the answer choices that you know are incorrect. For example, this will let your guess be a 1 in 3 chance instead.

What Your Score Means

Based on your score, you may, or may not, qualify for credit at your specific institution. The current ACE recommended score for this exam is 46. Your school may require a higher or lower score to receive credit. To find out what score you need for credit, you need to get that information from your school's website or academic advisor.

You lose no points for incorrect questions so make sure you answer each question. If you don't know, make an educated guess. On this particular test, you must answer 104 questions in 90 minutes.

Test Preparation

How much you need to study depends on your knowledge of a subject area. If you are interested in literature, took it in school, or enjoy reading then your study and preparation for the literature or humanities test will not need to be as intensive as that of someone who is new to literature.

This book is much different than the regular CLEP study guides. This book actually teaches you the information that you need to know to pass the test. If you are particularly interested in an area, or feel that you want more information, do a quick search online. We've tried not to include too much depth in areas that are not as essential on the test. It is important to understand all major theories and concepts listed in the table of contents. It is also important to know any bolded words.

Don't worry if you do not understand or know a lot about the area. With minimal study, you can complete and pass the test.

One of the fallacies of other test books is test questions. People assume that the content of the questions are similar to what will be on the test. That is not the case. They are only there to test your "test taking skills" so for those who know to read a question carefully, there is not much added value from taking a "fake" test. So we have constructed our test questions differently. We will use them to teach you new information not covered in the study guide AND to test your knowledge of items you should already know from reading the text. If you don't know the answer to the test question, review the material. If it is new information, then this is an area that will be covered on the test but not in detail.

To prepare for the test, make a series of goals. Allot a certain amount of time to review the information you have already studied and to learn additional material. Take notes as you study; it will help you learn the material. If you haven't done so already, download the study tips guide from the website and use it to start your study plan.

Legal Note

FLASHCARDS

This section contains flashcards for you to use to further your understanding of the material and test yourself on important concepts, names or dates. Read the term or question then flip the page over to check the answer on the back. Keep in mind that this information may not be covered in the text of the study guide. Take your time to study the flashcards, you will need to know and understand these concepts to pass the test.

Primary audience

Secondary audience

Semitechnical presentations

Internal document

External document

Technical brief

Primary sources

Secondary sources

Any other people who later come in contact with the material

The people who need the information and will use it to make decisions

One that is intended to be used only within the company or organization that prepared it

When the anticipated audience is familiar with the topic, but has less experience, specialized training, or expertise with the subject than the writer

A worksheet used to organize and summarize the likely readers' characteristics and needs

Written for readers that do not work for the company that prepared the document

Include material that other people have drawn from primary sources

Offer firsthand experience with the subject

RFI

Inside Address

Letters of Complaint

Letters of inquiry

Subjective descriptions

Objective descriptions

Process Narrative

Process Analysis

Includes the name, title, company, and address of the intended recipient

Ace The Clep

Requests for information

Ace The Clep

Requests for information about a service, product, person, policy, procedure, or organization

Ace The Clep

Sent when the writer is dissatisfied with a product or service

Ace The Clep

Based on facts, not opinions

Ace The Clep

Based on opinion

Ace The Clep

A subject-oriented description

Ace The Clep

Describes the process from the writer's point of view

Ace The Clep

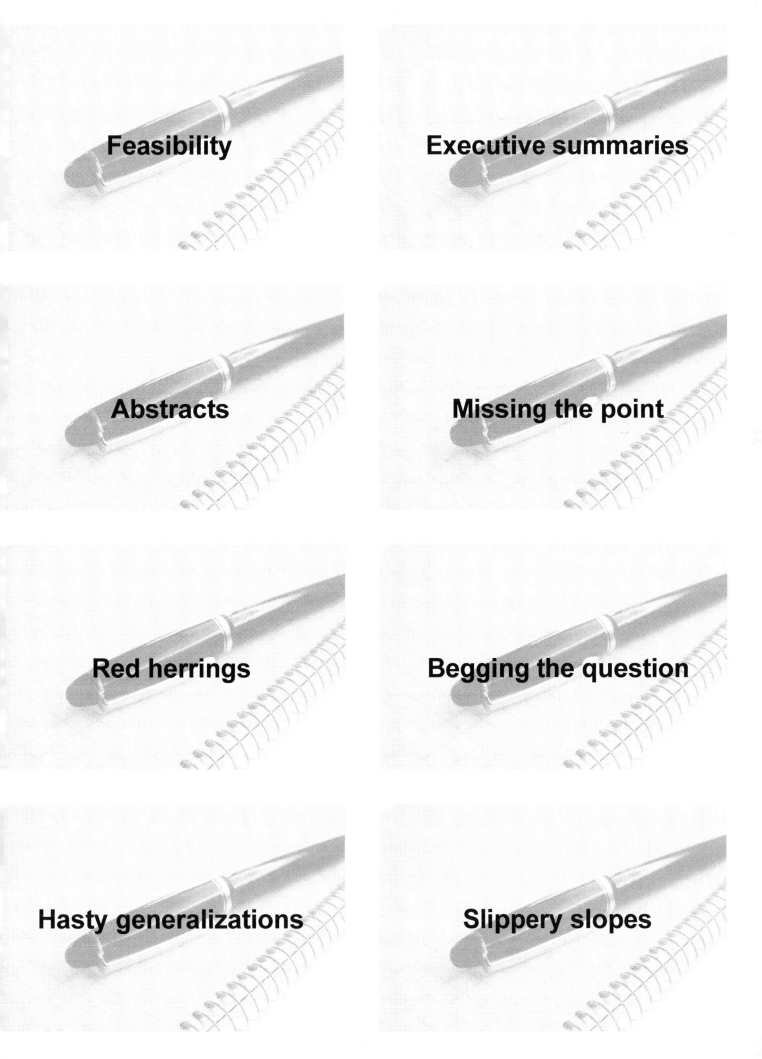

Feasibility

Executive summaries

Abstracts

Missing the point

Red herrings

Begging the question

Hasty generalizations

Slippery slopes

Used in business
proposals and reports

Examination of the
likelihood of success if
the proposed solution is
adopted

To draw a conclusion that
is more extreme than the
evidence supports

Common in scientific and
research documents

To base a conclusion on a
piece of information that is
essentially a restatement of
the conclusion or to ignore
flaws in a core piece of
information

A tangential issue that
is addressed in order to
distract the readers from
the main problem

Assumes a chain of events
will happen, even though
the evidence does not
support the entire chain

A conclusion based on
a sample size that is too
small or limited

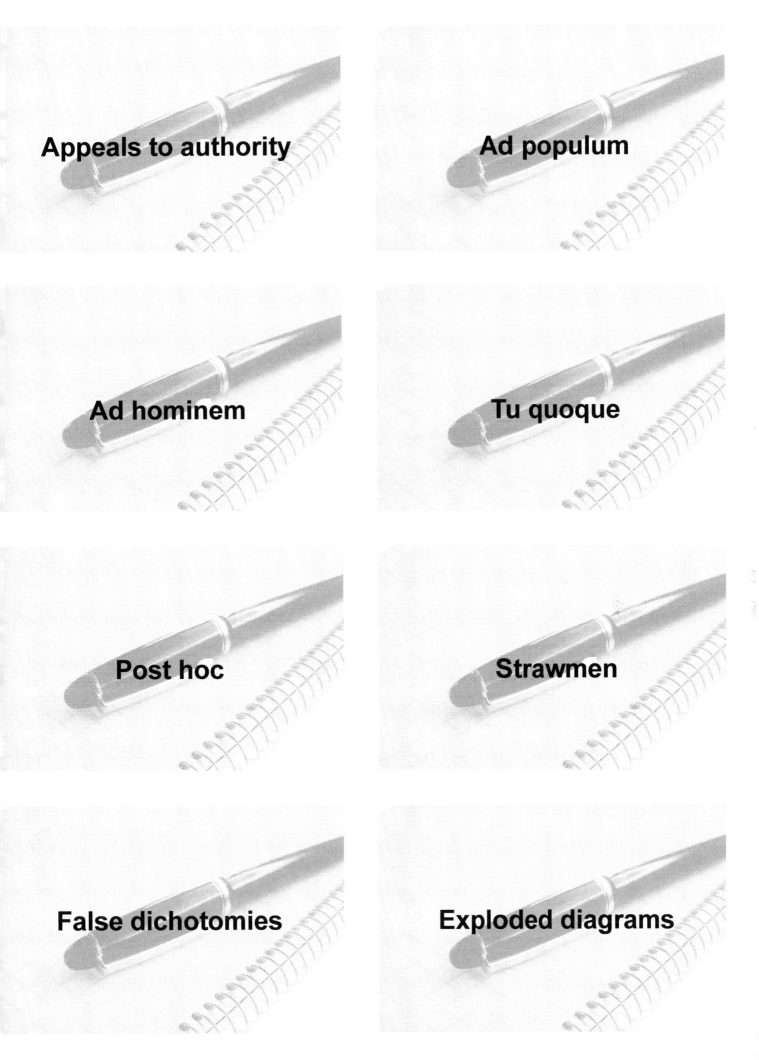

Appeals to authority

Ad populum

Ad hominem

Tu quoque

Post hoc

Strawmen

False dichotomies

Exploded diagrams

("to the people") argument relies on public opinion to support a position

Can take two forms: citing a person who is not an expert in the subject being discussed or failing to describe the reasons that support an expert's opinion

("you too") attack points out the hypocrisy of a person who supports a dissenting position

("against the person") argument attacks a person who supports a dissenting position, rather than the position

Are built when a watered down or misrepresented version of one side is described and then attacked

Assumes a causal relationship between two events

Show the details of how parts of an object fit together

The mistaken view that there are only two possible solutions to a problem

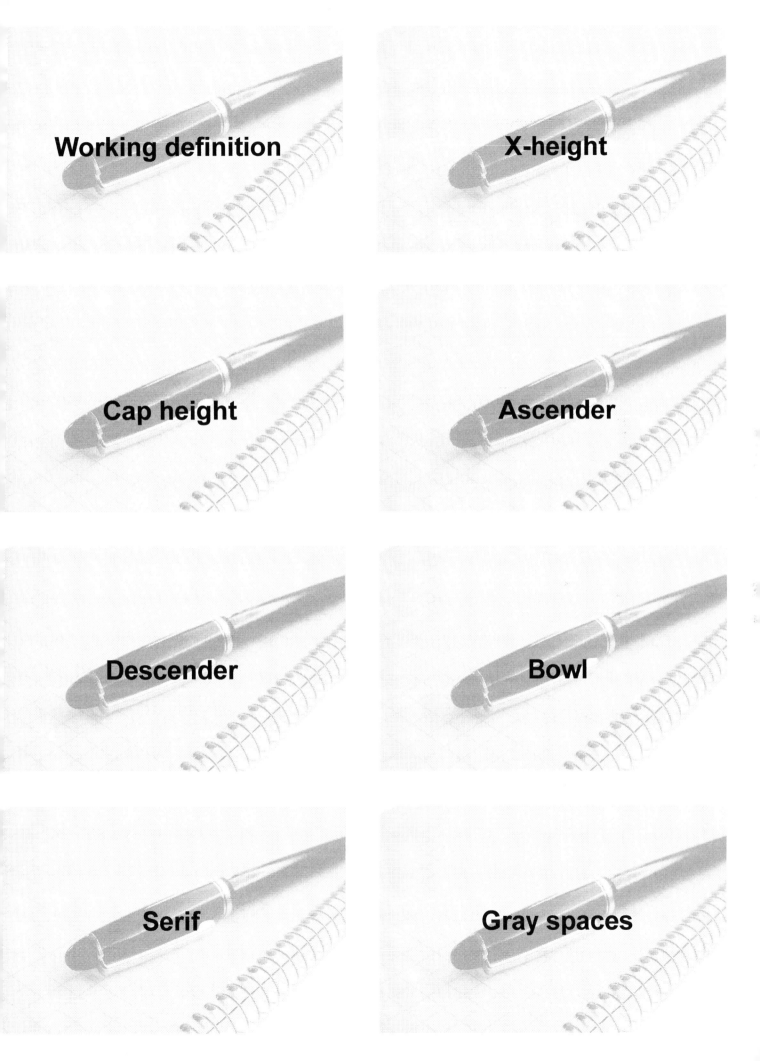

The height of a lowercase x, which reflects the height of the main bodies of the lowercase letters

A simplified description of a term

The height of the segment of lowercase letters such as h, d, f, and b that rises above the x-height

The height of the uppercase letters

The empty space inside letters such as Q, O, and D.

The height of lowercase letters such as p, j, y, and q that falls below the baseline

Areas that are occupied by text

Decorative strokes at the top and bottom of letters

Black spaces

Archaic terms

Jargon

Independent clause

Subordinate clause

Compound sentence

A compound-complex sentence

Unity

Words and phrases that are not generally used in modern communication but were common in previous decades

Hold graphics

A clause that can stand alone as a sentence if punctuation is added

Specialized language used in a field of study or profession

Contains two or more independent clauses

A clause where the predicate begins with a subordinate conjunction or relative pronoun

The extent to which the elements of a document develop a shared idea

Formed by at least one subordinate clause and two or more independent clauses

Made in the USA
San Bernardino, CA
23 January 2020